Marian Finucane:
The Saturday Interviews, 2005–2011

Marian Finucane:

The Saturday Interviews, 2005–2011

Edited by Luke Dodd

WOLFHOUND PRESS

Wolfhound Press
33 Fitzwilliam Place
Dublin 2
Tel: +353 1 278 5090
Fax: +353 1 278 4800
www.wolfhoundpress.com

© Marian Finucane, 2011

ISBN: 978-0-86327-973-7

Printed in Ireland by Colorman Ltd.

For Michael Littleton (1938–2002)

Contents

Introduction

I got my big break in RTÉ in the late 1970s when I was offered a post as a reporter on *Day by Day*, a summer programme which was presented by Pat Kenny. I had been at the station for several years before that working as an announcer, but it had always been my ambition to become a reporter. My work on *Day by Day* consisted of going out and about to do daily reports on topics as diverse as farming, the horse-breeding industry, pollution, disability and trade unions. It was bliss! Very quickly I came to realise how effective a medium radio actually is. I remember interviewing a young prostitute on her first night on the street. Her story – the fear, the resentment, the powerlessness – brought a flood of compassion from many of our listeners.

After my stint on *Day by Day*, I presented *Women Today*, and this is when I did my first live interviews. I think it's fair to say that much of the profound social change which Ireland has undergone in the last few decades relates to women's issues, which is of course to say issues that affect everyone. Ireland in the 1970s was a very different place, and would be almost unrecognisable to us now. Contraception and divorce had not been legalised, children born out of wedlock were classed as "illegitimate", the idea of equal pay or equal opportunity was only beginning to be mentioned, immigration was minimal and the power of the clergy was still largely unchallenged. In retrospect, it was a wonderful time to be working in broadcasting, a real privilege. Over the years, I've worked in all areas of television and radio – current affairs, religious programming, documentaries. But my real love is radio and in particular the weekly in-depth Saturday interview which has been part of my weekend programme since 2005.

All radio programmes are the result of teamwork – a relatively small group of people working intensely under the baton of the series producer, in my case Anne Farrell. The producers and researchers approach potential interviewees about coming on the show and, if they agree, the researcher will begin to work on a brief. As an interviewer, you like to know as much as possible about the subject, often much more than you will use in the interview. As well as the facts, anecdotes are really useful – they can enliven an interview that is overburdened with statistics or technical information, and they can put a nervous interviewee at his or her ease. The ideal preparation for an interview is to have a good idea of what the answers to your questions are going to be before you ask them.

In an interview I have to hand a sheaf of briefing notes prepared by one of the researchers – usually heavily annotated. These notes may well have gone through numerous drafts in the days leading up to the interview, as the researcher, producer and myself discussed the best angles, the best anecdotes and the most searching questions. Having a fixed set of questions in a specific order is not my preferred way of working. The interview has to be organic enough to allow you to take a different tack if the guest heads off in an interesting direction.

It makes very little difference whether or not I have anything in common with an interviewee or whether or not I like them. They have taken the time to come on the show and deserve the opportunity to be heard – they deserve respect. This, obviously, does not mean that they deserve an easy ride!

The interviewee is shown into the studio as the news headlines at the top of the hour are being broadcast. Once we go live and the red light comes on, I do my usual round-up of the newspaper headlines. I often wonder what goes through a guest's head as I do this, but I'm fairly sure it helps some at least to get comfortable.

The radio studio is a wonderfully intimate space. There, it's just me and the interviewee facing each other across a small desk with little outside interference, two people making a connection and in turn connecting with the listeners. Generally speaking, the interviews last about forty minutes with one commercial break. To have the best part of an hour alone with somebody for an interview is pretty unusual in broadcasting these days. It allows for an exchange that is entirely different to news and current affairs programmes, where the tone often has to be more urgent and adversarial.

For a lengthy interview, it is important to put the interviewee at his or her ease quickly. I often tell them that listening to the radio is a solitary experience, that it's just them, me and the listener. I prefer not to meet the interviewee prior to doing the interview because it preserves a certain distance between us and makes for a more spontaneous exchange. If someone tells you a good yarn or joke, they are often disinclined to tell it to you again on-air, as they don't want to repeat themselves. And it pays not to become too chummy with an interviewee before you start because this can sometimes exclude the listener. But Ireland is a small place and inevitably some of those I have interviewed have been acquaintances or friends. My ambition in doing any interview is to try and ask the kinds of questions the listeners want to hear.

My preference is for a live interview. It adds an extra dimension, an edge, if you like; we only pre-record as a last resort. In the studio, I have no ability to edit or interpret what my interviewee is saying. Again and again, when reading the transcripts of the interviews in this book, I am struck by the profound difference between the spoken and the written word.* The spoken word is full of personal cadences, incomplete sentences, things half said. The written word cannot convey the all-important tone of voice. A listener will immediately grasp the meaning implied by a drop in tone, a pause, a silence.

The most difficult part of doing this book was selecting the twelve interviews. Clearly there were dozens of wonderful interviews to choose from, although, inevitably, certain interviews did not transcend their particular time or context. And it was easy to exclude some of those interviews with public figures, where the interview consisted largely of waffle, evasion and the stringing together of platitudes. No overall theme emerged in the selection, although many deal directly with the big events that have

---

* To render some parts of the interviews suitable for print, minimal changes have been made. These changes are clearly indicated. The interviews are available in full on the RTÉ website: www.rte.ie.

shaped Ireland over the past decade or so – the rise and demise of the Celtic Tiger, sex-abuse scandals and the Church, immigration, etc. But it is the human stories that resonate the most deeply, and the age-old themes of love, suffering and death.

I would like to express sincere gratitude to Anne Farrell, the series producer who created the format of the programmes at the outset, and the co-producer Hugh Ormond. Thanks to the researchers and broadcast coordinators, and to those others who came and went from the team since the beginning. Thanks also to RTÉ. A big thank you to all of the people who have made themselves available for interview through the years, in particular those included in this book. And, most importantly of all, thanks to the listeners. Ultimately, it's all about the listeners.

Marian Finucane,
September 2011

1

Michael O'Leary, 28.11.2009

"Market forces dictate..."

When I started my first job as an architectural assistant in the 1970s my monthly salary was £58, and the average cost of a flight between Dublin and London – then the busiest route in Europe – was £216. Michael O'Leary of Ryanair, along with businessmen Tony Ryan and Peter Sutherland, is generally credited with breaking what was effectively a cartel operated by Aer Lingus and British Airways and thereby making cheap air travel available to all. In doing so, he invented a new flying experience – the no-frills airline – which has now become more or less the norm, irrespective of who you fly with. However, Ryanair's singular and unrelenting drive to refine the reality of "no-frills" flying often provokes vitriolic criticism. To some, he is clearly a hero; to others, a so-and-so and chancer who hides endless hidden charges behind seemingly cheap airfares. Irrespective of your view, Ryanair is now one of the largest airlines in the world and is one of the great success stories in Irish business over the past generation.

I often fly with Ryanair, as, indeed, can any lowly architectural assistant these days. Of course, I've had my little hiccups — like the time I was barred from a flight from Cork to Dublin because I didn't have a passport. As I approached the Ryanair desk, I was greeted warmly with smiles and "Howaya Marian. What has you in Cork?" We chatted about something I was doing for the Department of the Taoiseach (Bertie Ahern's tenure) and then they asked me for my passport. No passport. I mumbled pathetically that I wasn't a terrorist and the ticket had been bought by the Department of the Taoiseach, so they probably didn't think I was a terrorist either. No go. I came back with Aer Arann some hours later. But I've travelled Ryanair many times without any hiccup at all.

It took a long time to get Michael O'Leary on the show; largely, I suspect, because he genuinely likes nothing better than spending his free time with his family on the farm where he lives in Mullingar, and the last thing he wants to do is come to Dublin for an hour-long interview at the weekend. When he arrived in the studio, a familiar figure obviously, he was polite and courteous, but remote. He refused all hospitality and maintained a stony silence until he was shown into the studio. We shook hands, but he clearly didn't look or feel relaxed – the expression "coiled spring" came to mind. I don't spend much time with an interviewee before the interview starts. This is a conscious decision in order to maintain a degree of spontaneity and a bit of an edge. Michael O'Leary's body language was a perfect illustration of cautious tension. Presumably, combative is his default mode for most of his encounters with the media – he was on enemy territory!

I started the interview with a statement about the amount of tax he pays – rumoured to be €14 million in 2003 – and whether he was ever tempted to become non-resident as a way of paying less tax. He launched into one of his characteristic wide-ranging diatribes, head down, no eye contact.

MF: With all the talk at the moment about cuts and increases and taxes and all of that, I'm [reminded of a] couple of years ago, I think it was in 2003, when you waved a cheque that you had paid the Revenue, which at the time I think was [for] €14 million. Were you ever tempted to live offshore for taxation purposes?

MO'L: I think yes is the answer, but I don't think it would suit either my work circumstances at the moment, where I'm fully involved in running Ryanair, or my family circum-stances, where I [am], you know, married with three young children and we live in Mullingar. But, you could certainly foresee [me doing so], I think, in the next couple of years, unless this Government gets its act together and does it quickly. […] I think I'd take a view that if the tax is less than 50 per cent; if, for every extra buck I earn, I've gotta pay half to the Government for services – yeah, I think that's fair. I think when it starts to get to 60 per cent or 65 or 70 per cent, then I think "No" and I will seriously look at, I think, moving offshore […]. I don't mind paying. I'm probably one of the biggest taxpayers in this country. On an annual basis, I pay millions in tax. I don't regret it. I don't begrudge it, but I bloody well expect that if I'm going to spend this amount of money in tax then we're going to get some decent services in this country and some able political leadership, which we certainly don't have at the moment.

MF: It surprised me because I thought that the reason that you hadn't taken that option was bordering on an Irishness reason, you know, [that Ryanair is] an Irish company based in Ireland and that you liked the idea of being in Ireland and the kids being Irish.

MO'L: Ah, I do and [...] I would be very committed [...]. I'd like to see the kids grow up in Mullingar in a kind of a country setting on a farm, as I did. [...] [B]ut it would be unfair to say that, you know, I'm prepared to live in this country and pay tax come hell or high water – I'm not. I'm prepared to pay tax if I think there's reasonable equity in the tax system, and I think once tax gets above 50 per cent, in any case if the Government's going to take more than half of what you earn, even if it's on the incremental dollar, then I think it's not fair and I would seriously look at moving abroad. I hope it won't happen, but, you know, unless there is better leadership in this country than there has been for the last ten or fifteen years, it may well happen.

I pushed him on his views about political leadership.

MF: Where do you see leadership within the political system at the moment?

MO'L: [...] [I]n a bizarre way, if you look back, certainly in my life for the last thirty years, where do you see leadership? I think Haughey – and it's very fashionable to be very critical of Haughey, who was clearly a bit of a crook, but, God, was he able to get things done! You look at Government Buildings – you know it's terrific. The IFSC [Irish Financial

Services Centre] is terrific. But he was somebody at least who would make a decision and he would drive it through, over, I would say, the lethargy and incompetence of the senior civil service, and I think the senior civil service is probably more incompetent in this country than the politicians. I am a great fan of Charlie McCreevy. I think McCreevy was one of the best ministers for finance we've had here in recent years, again, because I think he ignored the dumbos in the senior civil service whose instinct is always, "You can't do that, Minister! You can't do that. You can't do that...."

Strange to hear Michael O'Leary wax lyrical about Government Buildings, dismissed by many as a Haughey vanity project and a waste of money, given his trenchant views on the second terminal at Dublin Airport, built by the Dublin Airport Authority (DAA), which he said had cost too much to build (Ryanair had offered to build this at its own cost). We moved onto the topic of capital gains tax and a possible increase in the rate, which was being mooted at the time. Again, he launched into a spirited defence of keeping the lower rate. He said the problem was that the Government had not introduced cuts. He referred with some admiration to Colm McCarthy's "Bord Snip Nua" report, which included another broadside attack on the Dáil: "And what did the Government do? They buggered off on holidays!"

I was a bit surprised to hear him supporting one of the recommendations in the report, namely, a cut to funding for horse racing – one of the much-publicised pleasures of Michael O'Leary's life. I realised that, unless I changed tack, the interview would end up being little more than an extended diatribe against the Government or an advert for Ryanair. I had to reassure him that I wasn't necessarily hostile to him. Michael O'Leary is used to short, sharp, adversarial exchanges with the media, but we had time together, so…horses.

> MF: When you're speaking about [horse racing], I just checked up a couple of names [of your horses] this morning: War of Attrition, Wings of War, Warfront, Warhead, War of the World – [there's a] certain commonality in those names.

He laughed. The atmosphere in the studio changed visibly. Every cell in his body seemed to relax. He looked at me, rather than at the desk, from then on. After the show, Anne, my producer, told me that the change was palpable from the control room!

> MO'L: Some clever wag said, […] "He's never going to name a horse 'Peace' [or] 'Tranquillity'." […] So, actually, I have two young horses coming along […], one named Peace and the other named Tranquillity.

> MF: Have you?

> MO'L: Yeah. They'll probably be useless, mind you, but…

> MF: Why did you go with the war theme?

> MO'L: In all fairness, because […] my brother Eddie, who buys the horses for me, we bought War of Attrition – and he was already named – from a guy, a friend of ours, called Ger Hourigan down in Tipperary. He turned out to be a marvellous horse. He's won the Gold Cup.

> MF: He's running today, I gather.

MO'L: He's running today, but he's a bit like myself now – he's getting older and slower, so he doesn't run quite as fast as he used to. But, you know, if you've that much luck first time out, you think, "Well, Christ. Let's call them all War-something-or-another!" It hasn't been quite so successful with the others, but you know…

MF: This isn't a statement of personality by any chance?

MO'L: I am sure, with all the personality flaws I have in my deformed and God-help-me personality, I'm sure there's something in it. But, no, it was because we thought we were lucky the first one was called War. We're actually running out of War names at this stage, so we'll probably have to move on to Peace and Tranquillity.

MF: Okay. There was a very nice story […] about you in your early days in Crumlin or Walkinstown….

MO'L: Yeah.

MF: And it was about the shop that you had that […] had turnover of about £1,000 a day. […] I'm quoting this now as I say, "…and being a greedy little bugger like I was at the time, we decided we'd open on Christmas Day."

MO'L: That's true.

MF: The staff objected.

MO'L: They did object, but one was my younger brother and the other was my younger sister, so you know their objections were promptly overruled.

MF: And, on the day, your turnover went up […]. What did you do?

MO'L: It was amazing. […] [W]e decided to open Christmas Day on Walkinstown roundabout − the shop has since closed; well, I sold it and it has since closed. We opened up on Christmas Day. It had never been done before and […] we doubled the price of the batteries because I thought […], "Somebody's always stuck for batteries on Christmas Day." We doubled the price of the batteries on the day and doubled up on the batteries. We [were] sold out [of] all the batteries before 11 o'clock in the morning, sold out [of] all the big boxes of chocolates and sold out [of] all the fags, because everybody […] around the Walkinstown area at the time ran out of batteries, fags and chocolates on Christmas Day. Turnover went up by about − and we only opened for about four or five hours − but the turnover went up fivefold and it was one of the greatest days of my life.

MF: And perhaps an indication of […] your approach to business.

MO'L: I think it is. Look, you know, you're providing a service if you can open on Christmas Day. Nobody was forced to buy the batteries. Nobody was forced to buy the chocolates. We didn't increase the price of the chocolates or the cigarettes, but if you provide a service, everybody has a choice whether [they avail of] it or not. If I choose to double the price of batteries on Christmas Day and they sell out by 11 o'clock, I am right.

MF: And what if people say, "That's a bit mean on Christmas Day. [What about] [t]he Spirit of Christmas?"

MO'L: Now, look, I'm providing a service. If you want the Spirit of Christmas, you know […] the shop could be closed, I could be sitting at home on my backside and you'd have no batteries at all for your children. […] Given that I'm now married, I am dutifully obliged to buy flowers on Valentine's Day. The cost of flowers the day before Valentine's Day is obscene, but you know you go out and you buy because if you don't show up with the flowers on Valentine's Day you'd be dead for a month! […] Market forces dictate….

During the commercial break we talked about the big news story that day – the incident involving Tiger Woods crashing into a tree near his home amid rumours of marital trouble. O'Leary remarked dryly that Woods must have forgotten the flowers! He was now hitting his stride. His various answers, all lengthy and very articulate, were peppered with frequent rants and broadsides. Throughout the course of the interview, he referred to senior civil servants as "dumbos", and "utterly, utterly useless"; politicians as "idiots"; Bertie Ahern as "that feckless ditherer" who tried "to be all things to all men"; the proposed tourist tax as "insane"; the Irish Government as "clowns"; the Equality Authority as a "complete bloody waste of time"; the National Consumer Association as "complete bloody rubbish"; trade unions as operating on the basis of "a narrow vested interest"; supporters of social partnership as worthy of shooting; the Senate as a "bloody useless talking shop", adding that his dog had more influence than senators. He clearly relishes the opportunity to air his contrary views and, to be fair, most of the calls to the show that day were openly supportive of much of what he said.

I asked him about his sometimes controversial advertising campaigns, in particular ads made at the expense of Mary O'Rourke TD and the Pope.

> MF: [In 2000] you ran a series of ads – you run great ads it has to be said – based on the remark Mary O'Rourke made about being in her bath,[1] just after her husband had died. Wasn't that a bit savage?
>
> MO'L: In actual fact, it was before her husband had died, but [...] we ran the ad about her the day after she said on radio that she heard about the resignation of Brian Joyce [as chairman] of CIE in her bath. Like, you run these ads because they're topical. [...] [W]ould we have run the ad if we'd known that Enda [her husband] had died? No, clearly not. But you run an ad the following day because it's topical and I'll say, actually, Mary got more publicity out of that bath. I mean more people remember Mary O'Rourke for the bath ad than for anything she did in her period as transport minister, you know, [...] when her list of achievements is tiny as transport minister. But [...] you would never knowingly run an ad [...] against a politician if you knew some member of their family had died. You run an ad because it's topical and it was topical; we ran the ad.

In the other ad that provoked widespread offence an image of the Pope appeared under a banner proclaiming, "Exclusive – Pope reveals Fourth Secret of Fatima". The Pope was shown whispering, "Psst! Only Ryanair.com guarantee the lowest fares on the internet" to a kneeling nun. It provoked widespread offence.

> MF: And I remember the "Fourth Secret of Fatima"....

MO'L: That was phenomenal. I mean, it's extraordinary what you get away with. We ran that ad on the Fourth Secret of Fatima expecting, you know, the usual: [...] somebody would ring in to Joe Duffy or Gay Byrne, or whoever it was at the time, complaining that we were slagging off the Catholic Church. My mother would call me and give out that we were slagging off the poor Pope or something! But we didn't get much of a spin and then the Vatican Press Office, about two weeks later, issued a press release condemning the Irish Catholic airline Ryanair for [using] a picture of the Pope. The ad ran round the world. *Los Angeles Times*. *New York Times*. *The Hindustan Times*. We got about €5 million worth of free publicity for one ad that cost us four hundred quid.

MF: And that's the thinking, is it, that if you go close to the wind, people will react and consequently the value will ratchet up?

MO'L: In actual fact, [...] with our ads we're not trying to go close to the wind. We genuinely are trying to be funny or entertaining, or humorous. You know, we ran ads last week on Thierry Henry handling the ball,[2] you know, which was "Hands off the French! Five quid fares to France. Get your own back!" Some of them work. Some of them don't. But the intention of the ads is never to be − I mean, with the exception of the ones [...] we run with the politicians in mind − the intention of the ads is never to be [...] personally wounding or offensive; it's genuinely to try to be entertaining. Now, some people might think we have a weird sense of humour, but you put, you know, about five or six [...] people together in their mid-twenties − this is their humour.

MF: So you don't go through an advertising agency *per se?*

MO'L: No. No. I mean we would never use an advertising agency. We don't use consultants. Anybody with a ponytail would get shot before they'd get in the door of Ryanair and we don't waste that kind of money. We think. [...] [I]f our people can come up with a humorous and/or topical ad, we'll run it.

There is no doubting that Michael O'Leary adores being the CEO of Ryanair. And I believe him when he says that he has no interest in a Seanad seat, living as a tax exile, appearing as a judge on *The Apprentice* and being awarded honorary doctorates ("those bloody baubles"). Listening to the interview again, there is a persistent self-deprecation in his tone, which those of strong and strident opinions often use to soften their message. But for all his bluster and rhetoric, he displayed a strong sense of social justice, both in terms of his own willingness to pay tax (albeit at no more than 50 per cent) and outrage at the way in which opportunities were squandered by the Government. When I asked him about the Celtic Tiger years he was particularly strident in his response.

MO'L: We've come through ten magnificent years because of, I think, [...] McCreevy reducing tax [and] Albert Reynolds, to be fair to him, about fifteen years ago getting about €16 billion[3] off the European Union and taking the dead hand of the civil service out of running the economy. [...] [T]he German bankers run the economy. And it's been a terrific fifteen years, but what have they done in those fifteen years? We put no money aside. We haven't addressed health services. The health service is a shambles despite throwing phenomenal amounts of money at it – huge overstaffing in it. [...]

[N]ow that we're in a recession, what money have we got, apart from the money that McCreevy put into the National Pension [Reserve] Fund? They've pissed it all away! And then because we had some feckless ditherer like Bertie here for the last five or ten years. And people are looking around for someone to blame in this country. We should all [...] blame ourselves! We elected Bertie Ahern three times [...]. Three times in a row. Fine maybe the first or second time. After that, it was quite clear all he would do was pander to the trade unions, buy off the vested interest [groups], anything at all. We deserve exactly what we get in this country at the moment because we elected that feckless ditherer three times.

MF: Have you met him often?

MO'L: Bertie? About two or three time.

MF: And did you say, "Good morning, feckless ditherer." Or did you say, "Good morning, Taoiseach"?

MO'L: [...] I don't think I'd say "Good morning" to him and I don't think he'd say "Good morning" to me either. The last time I met him, [I] could see the lips kinda getting all tight. I'd say he'd love to stick a knife in me if he could, although sadly he can't.

Michael O'Leary knows that he is by far the biggest publicity asset Ryanair has. He is media savvy, articulate and statistics roll off his tongue in a rapid-fire delivery that works to drown out everything else, particularly those with whom he disagrees. He comes across as eminently reasonable, and paints himself as the underdog fighting for the common man against almost insurmountable odds. But he can also be fast and loose with the facts – at one point in the interview he claimed that the average fare paid by Ryanair passengers using Shannon during "six months of the winter last year was €8". Later on in the interview, the €8 "average" Shannon fare was mentioned without any reference to the winter months. He was very quick to disparage a caller's remarks about how Ryanair's carry-on bags policy and internet-only booking system discriminates against older people – this at the same time as saying that he didn't have an online complaints service because "If you open up an email [channel] for complaints, you deal with more old crap and rubbish." One person's complaint is another person's "crap and rubbish"? I have a friend who was unable to use his Ryanair flight and applied in writing, as he was instructed to do, for a refund of the Government tax that was applied to the cost of the flight. In an *email* reply, he was told that the administration costs exceeded the cost of the refund.

Towards the end of the interview, when speaking about his "deformed and God-help-me personality", Michael O'Leary hints at a realisation that he might not be the best person to continue running Ryanair into the future, with an acknowledgment that somebody like him is good in a start-up scenario but that different expertise is required to get to the next stage. I was surprised to hear him say that he expected to not be running Ryanair in two or three years. I pressed him on that statement.

MO'L: Yeah, I think so. I think there are a couple of things left I'd like to get done. We're now the largest airline in the world. I'd like to break up the Dublin Airport Authority monopoly. I'd like to see the future of Aer Lingus resolved in the only sensible way it can be resolved and I think that's by putting it together with Ryanair. We should hand it over then to people who will run it, I think, in a more professional manner than I do, people who say the right things about the environment and customers and dogs and old people and everything else, because I'm just not that kind of person. I think what I do is very effective when you're growing Ryanair, but when you are the biggest airline in Europe you've got to be nice to politicians and regulators, and at that stage you need to take me out and shoot me!

As this book goes to print, he is still there at the helm of Ryanair.... And he had a winner in Cheltenham this year called First Lieutenant!

2

Gerald and Mary, 10.01.2009

"It's been very difficult sometimes to remind yourself that you have not done wrong..."

What happened to Gerald and Mary is every parent's nightmare. When their daughter was twenty she told them she had been abused by a priest – a good friend of the family – when she was fourteen. Their experience is one which, sadly, has many echoes throughout Ireland. Gerald and Mary did the live interview remotely from the RTÉ studios in Cork, a situation which we generally try to avoid. There is an intimacy about having the person (or persons) across the studio desk from you, an immediacy which can create an atmosphere of trust, particularly when the interviewee is nervous. But, in this case, that was not possible.

As I listen back over the interview I can hear an incredible air of dignified, controlled anger in the voices of both Gerald and Mary. Their simple, reasonable words are all the more remarkable when one considers the catalogue of accumulated betrayals and insults they were subjected to at the hands of the Church authorities. These are people of deep faith who have lived by a moral and ethical code – that of the Catholic Church – only to find that the Church hierarchy was very selective in applying those same codes to clerical wrongdoers. From the outset, Gerald and Mary are at pains to explain that their anger is directed at particular officials within the Church, not the Church itself. They are clearly a loving couple; they often talk in unison, one finishing the other's sentence.

> Gerald: I'm speaking on behalf of those that were abused because they don't have a voice; they haven't the courage; they're living in fear. [...] We're not here on a kind of a cleric-bashing...
>
> Mary: Exercise.
>
> Gerald: We're here to speak for the victims [...].

I asked them to explain how they had come to know the abuser.

> MF: You really liked this priest, didn't you? You respected him.
>
> Gerald: Yeah, [...] we were born and reared in the same parish. I'd have known his family very well, and they'd have been highly, highly respected farming people.
>
> MF: And you went out of your way, as I understand it, to attend his Mass because he gave a very good sermon.
>
> Gerald: Oh yes. He was popular and he'd have nice little anecdotes and stories and he could get across the message

very well. And […] you'd be supportive of someone you knew as well, you know. […]

MF: [Your daughter] used to go to his house for career guidance?

Gerald: He used go to the schools and he'd chat, and anyone who had any problems or wanted to know where they were going in life, you know, [he'd say for them] to pop into his house. He lives a hundred yards, a hundred and fifty yards, away from us. That was part of his recruiting system – […] he's very charming. The Bishop also told us that he was able to hypnotise people because [when we met with him] he actually asked our daughter was she hypnotised, and of course she said she didn't know. Apparently that was part of his *modus operandi* as well, and he'd ply the victims with drink, wine, and … I'm talking about young girls now.

MF: She was what age? About fourteen?

Gerald: Fourteen approximately.

MF: And he was plying her with wine?

Gerald: Yes.

MF: You must have been absolutely shattered when you discovered all this.

Gerald: It was an awful long time afterwards […].

Mary: She was about twenty when we would have become aware of it.

MF: And how did you become aware, Mary?

Mary: She told us herself. In conversation, it came out.

MF: You must have nearly keeled over.

Mary: It was an absolutely dreadful shock. Absolutely terrible. Devastating. I would never have believed such a thing could happen. Because we are practising Catholics and wouldn't have believed such a thing could happen.

MF: Well, I suppose, even when it happens, and you read about it, it's [about] somebody else. You never think it's going to come to your own door.

Mary: Yes. Absolutely. Yes.

MF: And was [your daughter] relieved that she could share it with you?

Mary: She would have been, but [...] even at that time we would have had absolutely no idea of the extent of his...

Gerald: Abuse.

Mary: His abuse. We [...] just had no idea until relatively recently how dreadful it was.

MF: And how did you find out recently?

Mary: Principally from...

Gerald: Another victim.

Mary: Another victim, yes.

Gerald and Mary's case happened in the context of a much wider investigation, now notorious, into the handling by Church authorities of abuse allegations in the diocese of Cloyne. In June 2008, Ian Elliott, the chief executive of the National Board for Child Protection, a body established by the Church hierarchy, completed a damning report into the Church's handling of abuse allegations in Cloyne, singling out Bishop John Magee and Monsignor Denis O'Callaghan for particular criticism. The report was published in December 2008. When Gerald and Mary did the interview, there had been growing calls for the resignation of Bishop Magee. They were adamant that he should resign, not only because of his failure to comply with the self-regulatory procedures agreed by the bishops, but because of their own experience of the Bishop when they met with him to discuss their daughter's abuse.

Gerald: My opinion of Bishop Magee, should he stay or should he go, [is that] his tenure to date is seriously flawed the way he handled things, the way he didn't handle things. He said himself that he made errors and he had failures, and that makes him, in my eyes, unfit to continue.

MF: Can I ask you about your initial contacts with the Bishop?

Gerald: Yes. I've been over this several times and it hurts every time I have to do it, I can assure you. We went with our daughter to the Bishop because this Fr D or Fr B […] – [there are] two different references in the two different reports on him – we wanted him out of circulation. It was as simple as that, because we knew and my daughter was aware that he was still recruiting and abusing. And we went to the Bishop and told him this. Now, when we […] mentioned Fr D, the number one reaction was "Are ye looking for money?"

MF: Was that the very first reaction?

Gerald: The very first time we met him when we said why we were there, his first question was were we looking for money […].

MF: How did that strike you?

Gerald: Maybe in a way it was a reasonable question to ask, because if we were looking for money it would be a legal situation, and I presumed he'd get his legal eagles in and we'd be speaking to them.

MF: Right.

Gerald: Then he spoke with our daughter privately for a few moments and we all came back together again in the room and he said, yes, he was confident that our daughter was telling the truth. […] And he then said that the priest, the particular priest, was acting very strangely, that he was in a curate's house in the parish he was in at the time and that they couldn't get him out, that he was refusing to leave the place. They wanted to move him somewhere else. Now, for what reason, I don't know….

MF: Right.

Gerald: But this is what he said to me – that the priest was behaving very peculiar – and he said, "This probably explains it."

MF: How would that explain it?

Gerald: The fact that he was abusing young girls explained his strange behaviour.

At the time that Gerald and Mary visited the Bishop they had no idea of the extent of the abuse and violence their daughter had suffered at the hand of her abuser – that was only revealed in the report that was sent to the Director of Public Prosecutions (DPP). They left the Bishop hopeful that their complaint would be taken seriously.

MF: When you went to the Bishop, and he obviously believed your daughter straightaway, what happened then, and what had you expected to happen?

Mary: […] As I already said, we had no idea of the awfulness of the whole business and we had felt relieved, I suppose. When we had laid it at his [door], we expected him to do what should be done […].

MF: And did you think of going to the Gardaí?

Mary: No. No. That might sound strange now, but you're going back a long time and it was the Bishop's responsibility. We presumed that he would deal with it, yes.

MF: So, what happened next? […]

Gerald: Nothing.

MF: Did the [Bishop's] office not get in touch with you?

Gerald: The Right Reverend Monsignor Denis O'Callaghan contacted us saying he was the Bishop's Delegate. I'd be up in every court in the country if I was to say what I thought of Father or Mr O'Callaghan. [...]

MF: And what procedures did they take, either in terms of your daughter or the priest, at that time?

Gerald: Initially he introduced himself and said he was the Bishop's Delegate and that he was dealing with this priest... this Father D, and he apologised and all the rest of it – he's a very plausible gentleman anyhow. He said he'd be in touch with us, and some time elapsed and he came back and told us that this priest had received some counselling and that he was now fine, and that there should be no more problem, that he was okay to be in ministry again as a curate.

MF: And how did you respond to that?

Gerald: I don't think I could repeat it.

MF: You sound far too gentle a person to [have said] anything excessive to him, but you indicated that you disagreed with him?

Gerald: Yes, and he assured me about the ongoing monitoring of the gentleman [...], but I know that it didn't happen.

MF: How do you know that?

Gerald: I have my little sources. We live in a very small rural area, you know. [He was seen] at race meetings in Mallow. He was there at the last meeting [...]. I'm not into the old horsey thing so I don't know, but last week or the week before he was seen at Mallow Races. And it's just that the whole thing is so difficult. On the one hand, you see, Marian, we're terribly loyal to the Church. And we're not about bringing anyone down; [...] certainly we don't want to damage the Church in any way, but the activity, the attitude of these clerics now – no wonder the Churches are empty. [...]

Returning to the issue of Bishop Magee's ongoing tenure and the behaviour of the Church authorities, Gerald added the following.

Gerald: And how in God's earth is he qualified? [...] Where are the Christians? I don't hear any Christian voice anywhere. The voice of Christianity, love and respect and and and...

Mary: Human decency.

And a little later on, Mary made another point that many people may have sympathised with.

Mary: I wanted to say, as well, with regard to the Bishop, that it must be tremendously difficult the burden that has been placed on the priests who are at the coalface. Does he think of them, the burden they are carrying, these men that give their lives to the service of God and of their fellow men?

Gerald and Mary's palpable disillusion with the officers of the Church was the result of a long, painful process. They were subjected to repeated demoralising and bullying behaviour, yet, somehow, they kept alive an unshakable belief in good. As if the inaction of the Bishop and Monsignor was not enough, the abuser threatened to sue when he became aware of their daughter's allegations.

MF: This priest approached you, is that not correct, and said that he was going to sue you?

Mary: Yes, that's correct. I was terribly frightened, I remember.

MF: You were frightened?

Mary: I was. It's a long time ago. I was very frightened.

MF: Because, on the other hand, if he did, it would have given you an opportunity to highlight the wrong that was done to your daughter?

Mary: Yes. You wonder though…these people seem to have access to a law that is different to the law that serves the rest of us. […]

MF: I re-read the [National Board of Child Protection's] report this morning and I have to say it could make you very, very angry. Have you had any further contact with the Bishop in recent times?

Mary: No. None.

MF: Or Monsignor O'Callaghan?

Mary: None whatsoever.

MF: I suppose, in fairness, we should point out they did assist her in getting psychiatric care, didn't they, counselling?

Mary: Yes. I suppose so. Yes.

Gerald: She had six sessions and when that was completed they wanted to see her file. They wanted all the intimate details that my daughter would have shared with the psychologist.

MF: But they wouldn't be entitled to that.

Gerald: No, but they looked for it, you know, but they didn't get it [...].

MF: All I can do is offer you my absolute deepest sympathy, as I suspect will most of the listeners listening to you, because, apart from anything else, given your commitment to the Church, given your faith, [we] can hear the hurt and the bewilderment [...] at how you've ended up in this situation.

Gerald: Yes.

Mary: Yes. And it's been very difficult sometimes to remind yourself that you have not done wrong, you know, that we have not done wrong. You have a feeling of shame, you know.

MF: Which, of course, is similar to what the victims feel too.

Mary: It is. Yes. Yes.

Bishop Magee eventually stepped aside in 2009 and his resignation was formally accepted by the Vatican the following year. In July 2011 the Commission of Investigation into the Diocese of Cloyne published its report into how allegations against nineteen priests were dealt with between 1996 and 2009. In it, Bishop Magee was found to have lied about reporting all abuse allegations to the authorities. He was also mentioned as one of the nineteen priests identified by the Commission, for "inappropriate behaviour" towards an eighteen-year-old boy. Monsignor O'Callaghan explained his own lack of action by stating that he had sometimes become "emotionally and pastorally drawn to the plight of the accused priest". Cardinal Connell's citing of the Doctrine of Mental Reservation comes to mind, whereby Roman Catholics can withhold the truth if the greater good is served.

In the aftermath of the publication of the Cloyne Report, I heard one victim on the television say, "I feel as if I have been touched by the devil." The vitriol of Taoiseach Enda Kenny's statement in the Dáil in July 2011 on the publication of the Cloyne Report shocked many, but few took issue. How long will it take for the "dysfunction, disconnection, elitism – the narcissism – that dominates the culture of the Vatican" to change?

3

Dermot Bolger, 09.04.2011

"The important thing is to love or to be loved..."

Dermot Bolger, novelist, playwright and poet, arrived in the RTÉ studio with a lovely photograph of his wife Bernie. She had died in May of the previous year and he had agreed to talk to me about their life together, and the awful manner of her sudden death. There is nothing unique about his experience – people lose loved ones all the time – but there is something special in hearing somebody whose life is words explaining one of the most fundamental and common of all human experiences. The reaction to this interview was phenomenal – a friend referred to it as one of those interviews that people stop you in the street about. His loving, moving words need little context; he was a man and a poet coming to terms with the loss of his life partner.

Dermot talked with great affection and humour about his and Bernie's first meeting. From the beginning, Bernie maintained a distance from Dermot's writing, waiting until something was finished before reading it.

DB: We first met by fluke in 1984 in The International Bar [in Dublin]. I'd just come in the door and I was wearing a monkey hat – it was raining outside. And I'd taken my glasses off, because you know how when you walk into a pub your glasses steam up. And I met this beautiful girl in white jeans and I risked it and I said, "Would you like to go for a meal in the Trocadero?" When we got to the Trocadero I had to take off the monkey hat and put on my glasses and she discovered that she was with a prematurely bald fellow with glasses. But I told her that the blueberry cheesecake was beautiful and blueberry cheesecake is blueberry cheese-cake, so you put up with certain things.

Bernie was always losing things and she gave me her post to mind and forgot it. So the next day I cycled out to her house [with it] and, very quickly, we knew that we were for each other. But she never had an interest in me as a writer. I've never been a commercially successful writer, but I've knocked out a living with the thin sliver of my imagina-tion since the age of twenty-four – but that didn't interest her at all. She just liked me as a person, or disliked me as a person – there were bad days as well [laughs]. When I gave her my first book she hid it under the bed in case her father found it because she thought it was quite indecent. I remember going for a walk with her very, very early on and saying, "We'll probably never own a house if you stick with me because writers don't make much money." But she'd no interest in that side of things. So no matter what happened in my life, if good things or bad things happened, you went home and you were given a dishcloth and she said, "There's the dishes." You had fun and our world was us and the two boys – we had a small little independent republic of love.

Bernie called us her "three Ds" and what happened in that house had no connection to this other Dermot Bolger that people knew about....

MF: I was amused at the fact that [...] you told her that you had finished [*The Valparaiso Voyage*] – I think she hadn't seen [it] – and she said, "There will be a sex scene on page three."

DB: That's right. There used to be a lovely little restaurant called the Orange Tree in Maynooth, where we used to go – I think it's gone now. We were there having dinner and I said, "*The Valparaiso Voyage* is coming out next week." And she said, "Oh! That's great. That's great. Who wrote that one?" and I said, "No, love. Bernie, that's actually my book. That's the one that I've been writing out in the lighthouse in Howth for the last two years" [laughs]. And she says, "Oh! Yeah. I bet you there's a sex scene on page three!" And I said, "No, Bernie. No. There isn't. It would be great if you knew the name of the book, love, and there is no sex scene on page three." And then, of course, when I actually got the book from the printers, I realised that there was a small sex scene on page three. So, she sort of knew me better than she thought. But I liked that, I liked that the priority was us. And we had good years and we had bad years at home....

Dermot explained that after the birth of one of their sons Bernie had contracted glandular fever, which developed into ME. This had robbed her of a decade of good health. When her health was restored, she had embraced life with gusto. The day she died had, in many ways, been an ideal one.

DB: She had watched [a] double [bill of] *Coronation Street* on the Monday night, which was her great big thing in life. She was playing golf the next morning at the Eagles in Leopardstown. I loaded up her clubs the night before. She was in great form. She went off. She played with her friend Claire, who she loved playing with of all the people out there, because sometimes there were serious golfers and she would be a bit nervous around them. She just wanted to have fun. She had a wonderful morning. She met people that she hadn't met for a long time at lunch. She went out and played another nine holes. They came back. The sun was shining. She loved the sun. She was a very childlike woman in many ways. I came in and I said, "Listen, Bernie, the sun is shining. Go out to the back garden and sunbathe. I'll make dinner." I can still see her lying in the back garden, sunbathing […]. [That evening] she was bringing one of our sons swimming to the pool in Belvedere where she had friends. One of our other sons was going to the gym. I don't remember Bernie leaving the house. She was going to be back at eight o'clock. The lads would have pizzas. It was just a very ordinary day. She was working the next day – she worked as a relief nurse which meant that she was a bit like Batwoman; she'd be there waiting for the phone to ring. So she knew she had work the next day so, really, she was having the most perfect day of her life."[…] She enjoyed the sun. She was with her friends. She was swimming with her friends.

While Bernie was swimming she had two seizures, one in the water and one at the poolside. She was taken to Temple Street Hospital and from there to the Mater Hospital. When Dermot was contacted he initially assumed that she had had some kind of reaction to the day's exertions. What happened next is an experience that many of us will recognise – the nightmare of Accident and Emergency (A&E).

DB: The nursing care at the Mater is extraordinary, but you have to get through this thing called "A&E" first. I think that is the big thing in the Irish health service. If you get into hospital you're fine, but A&E is all squalor, a maelstrom. When I got to my wife, she was lying on a stretcher in a cold corridor, just wearing her swimming costume. She was terrified. She wasn't sure what was happening. She was delighted to see me. We had wonderful tender moments together and she said, "What's happening, pet?" And I said, "You've had a seizure." And she said, "What's a seizure?" And I said, "Well, you're the nurse, Bernie, so you'll have to tell me." There were no nurses [available] so the ambulance men explained things to me. She was there for six hours; she was vomiting in my arms an awful lot and I was trying to give her what comfort I could. And the nurses brought her off to have a brain scan. Even though I was with her, she was always asking, "Where's my husband?" And I said, "Holding your hand here, pet." The brain scan was clear. And the funny thing is, my wife was dying in front of me and I didn't know it and nobody in hospital knew it.

Dermot explained how he went into overdrive dealing with practical matters – taking Bernie's car home from the pool and settling his sons down for the night before returning to hospital.

DB: She was getting worse and worse. She was saying, "My throat is killing me." The doctor didn't seem to take this all that seriously. He had given her some painkillers – paracetamol – and she was saying, "I need something more." The doctor said maybe she banged her throat on the edge of the pool. Because of her head symptoms, they were waiting for another team to take over and, finally, at two o'clock in the morning, a nurse came and said, "Will you step outside the curtain and talk to a new doctor? He's taken over her case." And I was so thrilled, because this new doctor was exactly the doctor Bernie would have wanted in that he was really concerned for her. He was very, very practical.

The last thing I remember of Bernie was the nurse taking her blood and she was very distressed. She gave the nurse this radiant smile – she had a great radiance in her smile – and she was talking to the nurse about being a nurse herself, which she normally wouldn't do. There were no symptoms, Marian, you know, so I could have probably told the doctor in thirty seconds what happened, but I told him in three or four minutes. I talked too long. He relieved me greatly and said, "We'll bring her in and we'll get an MRI scan tomorrow" and [he said] that it would take a few days to get the results. Then he said, "I'll examine your wife." And we pulled back the curtains. She had been left alone in those couple of minutes and she died in front of my eyes and I had no idea why and the hospital had no idea why, and suddenly you go from talking about doing things next week to […] resuscitation. You're being pushed off into a little dark family room by yourself and you don't know if your wife is alive or dead, and it's a strange, strange place to be in. [I was there for] around twenty minutes. Then I had to go back and all of this was happening amid drunks and policemen and junkies, and, for such a dignified person, it's a very undignified place. But that's where the [A&E] staff have to work […].

MF: I know. I've been in there. A member of my family went through it.

DB: When I finally found my wife again, she was on this machine, but I knew she was dead. People would contact me then and say, you know, "My partner is dying of cancer" – and they've three months to live, or four months to live.

And which is worse − to see them go through that pain, or to have somebody have an absolutely perfect day and die suddenly at the end of it? But it's very hard when someone is fifty-one years of age, and in the best of health, to never say goodbye to them.

And one thing is − I'm Irish, and if you're Irish you have certain contacts. So I was able to go to certain medical people within a day or two and I was able to find out what happened to my wife. I found out that my wife had a dissecting ruptured aneurysm − an aneurysm that had ruptured in her throat. And normally, with this, the blood descends down through the layers and into the heart and gives you a heart attack, and this is what must have happened. But I think, possibly, because she was swimming, maybe because she was doing a tumble turn − I don't know, we'll never know − the blood also went up and flooded her brain and this gave her a seizure. I mean doctors can only follow the symptoms the patient presents with and the first symptoms were seizures, so they figured that it was like a brain haemorrhage or something. And so they were looking at her brain at the same time as she was actually dying from something totally different. But I was able to find this out within two days, not illegally, but through those channels that an Irish person will have. If you were from Lithuania or Latvia, or you were a migrant worker over here, you wouldn't know that. It took me nine months to find out, officially, why my wife had actually died.

Dermot's greatest regret is that they had never moved to a larger house, particularly when Bernie was suffering from ME. Apart from needing more space as their family grew up, there had been trying times with neighbours. However, his uncertain income from writing made it difficult to compete with the high earners in the boom years of the Celtic Tiger.

MF: You were, were you not, going to move house?

DB: We loved our house. It was a first-time starter home and I remember on the first night there was a knock at the door, a man called Chris Kelly, a wonderful old man, who lived in an old house behind us. James Joyce had lived in that house and Chris Kelly was an old printer who had printed the first edition of *Bungalow Bliss*[4] in a shed in the garden. I thought it was great that the two most important books in Irish culture, *Ulysses* and *Bungalow Bliss*, both came together there.

MF: A certain irony there.

DB: And the last week of his life, he brought [us] vegetables from his garden. The Celtic Tiger changed things and suddenly houses in Drumcondra were being bought by investors and landlords. We probably did need a bigger house, although when the kids were small it was right beside the school and the park. We had noise problems, and when someone's anxious or someone's ill you really want to protect them and wrap them in cotton wool. Maybe I was always trying to find the perfect house for her and that can be a bad thing. But I was always like those Irish runners in the Olympics who are leading on the first bend of the mile and think they're great, and don't know that there's a clatter of Ethiopians right behind them just waiting for the real race to begin. We lost at auction so many times. [You'd] be bidding against somebody and you'd be going over your asking price by €50,000 and €60,000, and finally you'd win and the other person would be in tears. You'd have won and then there'd be a guy doing Sudoku in the back row who wouldn't have even looked up, and he'd just bid by an extra €40,000 suddenly out of nowhere, and you would realise that the real auction had only just begun and you were wiped out. I'm one of the few people in the world [who] actually would love to be sitting here half a million euro in negative equity, because you could make half a million back, somehow, over ten years, but you'll never get your wife back and, so, I would have loved her to have had the dream house that she wanted or something, or a house where she had peace, but that's the nature of....

MF: And how are you now?

DB: I don't know. I'm okay. Sometimes I'm a bit like a ghost fulfilling contractual obligations. One is still able to function at a certain level. People always recommend the names of books to you and Ray Yeates, the actor, mentioned a book called *Who Actually Died?* I didn't need to read the book, but I knew suddenly that a part of me had died too. I wasn't the guy who wrote those ten novels or wrote those twelve or thirteen or fourteen plays, or whatever. That, really, my life had been built around the fact that [...] males die first. You're always terrified that you're going to die and that your family won't be looked after, particularly if you're a writer. It's a very insecure occupation, because you never know what cheque is going to come in the post. Samuel Johnson said that only a blockhead writes for any reason except money and, although my books or my plays were never ones that were going to make loads of money, they were written with the [object] that you had to make provision for your wife and your family, so suddenly [...] the purpose of [...] your life had changed.

In answer to a question about writing since Bernie's death, Dermot, with characteristic honesty and poignancy, mentioned how it had been the death of his mother when he was a child that had made him into a writer. He also explained that he found writing difficult since Bernie's death. And he was wonderfully ambivalent on the subject of an afterlife – what grieving person wouldn't want to hold out the hope that there might be some other place where they would, once again, meet their beloved?

MF: And have you been writing since Bernie died?

DB: I wrote one poem when Bernie died. A poem about Bernie. I'm not really writing. My mother died when I was ten years of age and I realised, years later, that that made me a writer, because when your mother dies, when something like that happens to you when you're very young, you invent a fictitious world. I invented this fantasy where she wasn't dead at all. It was a mistake. There was a mix up of bodies. There was a woman with amnesia. It was my mother wandering around Dublin and she would come to me in a week's time or two weeks' time, and it would all be right again. And then I realised this was what I just kept doing from the age of ten. I just kept inventing these fantasy worlds. You could invent this alternative reality. You could live in two worlds at the one time – the real world and then this world of all these phantoms of your imagination that became plays and novels or poems, or whatever.

My mother's death made me a writer. But when my wife died in front of my eyes – that killed that part of my imagination, because it was too real [and] there was nothing you could invent. [...] So, really, I haven't. In the last few weeks I've gone back to it... My sister's a very fine writer and [...], in addition to being a novelist, she's ghost-written some books as well. And almost like a ghost writer I can go back to some fragments of things that I had written before and I can begin to work on them. Maybe one day some cause or some person, or something, will give me the inspiration again. But, even though Bernie wouldn't have necessarily been the person who [...] read the books, she was the person they were written for; [they were] written in the hope that they would please her, or that she would enjoy them. She was the purpose of my life for twenty-five years.

MF: Do you believe in an afterlife?

DB: I don't know, Marian. I don't know. The problem with being a writer is that you understand how words work and you understand the comfort that words give, and you understand that words are written in smokey rooms by people. I don't want to give myself any false comforts.

MF: And you think that would be a false comfort, if you did [believe in an afterlife]?

DB: I think in some ways it's very, very hard to know. I respect people's faith and I know that a lot of people are praying for Bernie and a lot of people talk to Bernie, as a lot of people talk to their dead, no matter who their dead are. All over Ireland there are people who feel that the dead help them and maybe that is true. As a writer you have to have an open mind and basically my viewpoint is that I know nothing. I am the ultimate Manuel in *Fawlty Towers* and I'm hoping there is, but I can't say that there is.

MF: If you did [believe] would it make it easier?

DB: I think so. Yes. I think it would be nice. I think that lots of people have time to say farewell to the person they love and we didn't have that. It would be nice to think that there would be a conversation finished. But maybe the conversations are finished. Maybe you just need to go back and decode those conversations. Maybe it's like trying to end a play or a novel. I remember writing my first novel, and I realised after nine months of rewriting the last chapter that the novel had ended in the previous chapter and people didn't need to say the things they were trying to say. When I found Bernie lying on a stretcher in a freezing corridor and she said she loved me, maybe that's as good; maybe you don't need anything else after that, you know.

And on the subject of grief and how to cope with it, Dermot's words were among the most eloquent I've ever heard.

DB: You try to honour the memory of the person you loved and the people you loved. There are people today having arguments about absolutely stupid things, as we all have arguments about stupid things, and I think if there's anything you learn it is to stop fighting and give each other a hug, because there [will be] a time when you won't have a chance to do that. It's very easy to be wise after and say, "I should have bought this house or that house" or "I should have said this." Or, "We should have gone on a world cruise." But you're in the business of living your life. When you look back on the good times, the bad times — we had wonderful times together. We were very much in love. She was a very unique and special person and she made me very happy. Those are things that nobody can take away; they matter more than novels or plays or anything else. The important thing is to love or to be loved and I was both, and I was very lucky.

I know it's a cliché, but a few lines from that wonderful John Donne poem "No Man Is an Island" constantly came to mind as I re-listened to Dermot's simple and powerful words: "any man's death diminishes me, because I am involved in mankind."

4

Mary Coughlan, 28.03.2009

"We were over-exuberant..."

A little over a month before Mary Coughlan agreed to come on the show an estimated one hundred thousand people took to the streets of Dublin to protest at the Government's handling of the financial crisis. Mary Coughlan was the Tánaiste and Minister for Enterprise, Trade and Employment at the time. She had been appointed by the new Taoiseach Brian Cowen after the resignation of Bertie Ahern in May of the previous year. The Government was in the process of imposing a pension levy on 350,000 public sector workers, and unemployment rates had risen to 326,000 in January, the highest number in a month since records began in 1967. Mary Coughlan had come in for some ferocious criticism in her new role, which she had held for about a year when she did the interview. On 1 March 2009, a few weeks before she did the interview, a very critical profile of her was published in the *Sunday Times* (Irish edition), which catalogued her numerous gaffes and failures, citing inexperience and an over-reliance on civil servants. It referred to her as "Calamity Coughlan".

It was a strange time for Fianna Fáil – the single most successful political party in Europe since the beginning of the twentieth century. They had presided over the halcyon days of the Celtic Tiger until the bubble began to burst in 2008. The general public turned on them with a vehemence that, for the first time, began to unravel the tribal loyalties on which the strength and success of the party was based. An *Irish Times* opinion poll put Fine Gael and the Labour Party ahead of Fianna Fáil – a new low.

It is now hard to imagine the old Fianna Fáil party ever being able to return to its pre-eminent position in Irish politics. It was always the party of political dynasties. The Government was led by a triumvirate – Taoiseach Brian Cowen, Tánaiste Mary Coughlan and the Minister for Finance, the late Brian Lenihan – who were all elected to the Dáil following the deaths of their fathers; Mary Coughlan at the age of twenty-one. More than one caller to the show that day – nearly all were hostile, I should add – linked the inherent paternalism and tribalism of the party to the financial disaster; the fact that, for Fianna Fáil ministers and TDs, the party came before the country:

MC: No. It's people first. We're elected. We have a mandate. It is the Government and the Government must legislate and the Opposition's job is to challenge that, one way or the other....

MF: As citizens watching the telly and watching what goes on in the Dáil, [it often comes across as] petty, pathetic sniping between political parties on political grounds, while the country's going down the tubes. People find it very hard to take and, on a number of occasions recently, when the Opposition offered some generosity it [was] dismissed.

MC: Well, first of all, we are in a coalition government. It's not a Fianna Fáil government. It's a coalition government supported by others. So, therefore, we have to clearly take into consideration their perspective and their points of view and I have to say we work very well. We have a programme for government. We work through that programme and we're elected on that basis. Secondly, I'm a Fianna Fáil person. I joined the Fianna Fáil party. Eamon Gilmore joined the Labour Party. You know, there's nothing wrong with belonging to your party or a framework....

MF: Of course there isn't.

MC: And having a philosophy and a way in which we work....

MF: What is that philosophy? What is the way you work?

MC: The way I work, in my view, is, firstly, I'm member of the Fianna Fáil party and I have to support my party members. I don't always agree with them and they certainly don't always agree with me. Secondly, I'm a TD from Donegal South West and I have to represent those people who have gone out for many, many years and supported me and I know their issues and their challenges, and it's my job to look after them and to support them. Thirdly, I'm a national politician....

MF: Thirdly!

MC: No. I'm just saying "first, second and third". You asked me. I'm a party person – yes. Do I represent my own constituency? Yes, of course I represent my own constituency. And I'm also a national politician. We're working on a programme for government. We're working within a coalition framework....

MF: Why do you think, then, there is that perception that you in particular put Fianna Fáil ahead of everything else?

MC: No, I don't. I put the people first. It's the people of Ireland that elect you. It's the people of Ireland we have to look after [...].

Toward the end of the interview, I returned to the issue of political dynasties, particularly within the Fianna Fáil party, and whether or not she thought they were healthy for the political process.

MF: And the notion that there's the "Coughlan seat" or the "Cowen seat" and that they are family seats.... Do you think that's appropriate?

MC: Well, there's no such thing. Even though, by its nature, for many years we've had a lot of family people. Both Brian [Cowen] and I, [as well as] Brian Lenihan [...], came into politics through the death of our fathers. People who are not in politics, I suppose, don't have a real realisation of the commitment and the sacrifice of political life. A name is hugely important especially in rural areas [...]. I remember when I made my speech in 1986, just shortly after Dad died, at the [Fianna Fáil] Convention, and I said, "This time I will be judged by my father. The next time I will be judged by my own actions." And that's been that way since 1989. [A name] is a help, but if you don't come up to the mark, the party and the people will not elect you.

MF: And, as a general principle, you don't have any difficulty about family seats?

MC: No, I don't, [but] what I would say is we always like to encourage new people to go forward, [in particular] more women to come into political life [...]. I'm glad to say that, for the local elections, we have 40 per cent new candidates coming through the system and that's great to see. And nobody has any right to a seat just because you are who you are. And now what you'll see, Marian, quite obviously, is, firstly, people are not in the Dáil or Senate for as long as they used to be and, secondly, not as many people are coming through the family route and that's good too. You have to give people who've an interest in public life the opportunity to go forward.

Taoiseach Brian Cowen had been on the show two months before. He and Mary Coughlan had rehearsed the, by then, familiar scapegoats for the Irish financial meltdown – the global crisis; the lack of liquidity in banking; the subprime mortgage crisis in the US; the weakness of sterling; the open economy, etc. Both were indignant that they had nothing to be sorry for. But, of the two, Coughlan was less trenchant and more forthcoming; generally speaking, she has a warm personality and friendly demeanour. They say she's great fun socially but, truth to tell, there wasn't going to be much fun in this interview given the state of the national finances. Occasionally, that other side of her personality did come through – a twinkle in the eye and that throaty laugh.

As with the Taoiseach, I pressed her on the allegation of Fianna Fáil's mismanagement of the economy and it's over-dependence on the building sectors. As is often the case with politicians, she had clearly come to the studio intent on taking criticism for lesser problems – in her case, lack of competitiveness and the high cost of energy in Ireland – as a way of deflecting criticism from much more significant areas. She raised these issues early in the interview, in response to a question about how a new minister gets on top of his or her new brief.

MC: When there's a change of government or a change of minister, each department puts together a portfolio of everything that's going on and you take in your secretary general and your assistant secretaries, and they go through each of those portfolios. Then you take this ginormous brief with you and you go through it yourself. I always find that reading things is fine, but being in a position where you can talk to people is much, much better; where you can question people, "Should we do this? Should we do that?" So, you're right in saying that I moved right across the road from the Department of Agriculture, Fisheries and Food, which I knew like the back of my hand, into a new portfolio which was, to some extent, different but [with] a massive variety of reading that had to be done. It is law, it's consumers, it's [trade] unions, it's employers, it's enterprise – it's all of these things. So I had to take the time to brief myself, work through it and then meet people. I took a lot of time to meet chief executives of foreign direct investment [FDI] companies [and] our own indigenous companies, being briefed by all of my State agencies, talking to people – talking to business people, consumers, meeting the unions — and it's by having that interaction, in my view, you actually learn and listen.

MF: You've all been on a steep learning curve.

MC: We have. And, you know, that concentrates the mind [...] and we've refocused [our minds in terms of] where we're at. Perhaps it was easier a number of years ago to invest, to look at business and look at different ways of doing things. [...] I think, in one way, it will refocus one of the huge issues that I have to deal with, which is competitiveness. Did we become lazy? Did we not use our heads as much as we should have, perhaps? So, now, we're sticking very closely [to the issue of] competitiveness. How we can reduce cost to business. How we can be more competitive. How we can attract more people to invest here. How we can support our own indigenous industries — and that's a key focus of the mind. And, as well as that, how we're going to be innovative. How we're going to do things better and more for less, as one might say.

MF: Can I go back to the point there? You go in, you meet the secretary general. We have all seen *Yes Minister*[5] How do you make the transition from being, as it were, taught and guided to being in charge and running policy?

MC: Well, every minister does that and you take from your experience how you do things. So [...] each minister has an overview of everything, and within every department, because there are fifteen people who sit around the [Cabinet] table and we listen and deliberate and talk, and give different perspectives to everyone else's departments [...]. And we're very strict in [operating within] government policy [...]. It's the intricacies of each part of the department [that] you need to [understand]. And what I did was to meet all of my agencies — we went through everything *ad infinitum*, spent a considerable amount of time going through [it] all. Then I take that and I [...] evaluate how it actually matches with the people I have to look after: the consumers, the unions, the employers and the business people. [...] And then I travelled to the States, for example, and met and got access to key people within the boardrooms. And, you know, we have a huge opportunity still and remain to attract people into this part of the world [and] to get new investments we have available to us, but we also listen to what [these investors are] saying. What are they saying about the Irish economy? What do they want?

MF: And what do they want?

MC: Well, what they want is, first of all, that we continue to invest in research and development. That we continue to invest in science and technology. That the 12½ per cent corporation tax is key, but people, people, people, skills, flexibility [...] and talent is what they want. And they've said to me, and I'm sure you've heard it yourself, Marian, *ad infinitum*, we need to encourage our young people to take up mathematics, to get into science, get into technology, and use that as a pathway to attract the FDI and, as well as that, create opportunities for themselves. [...]

MF: But we did let our costs go too high.

MC: We did and...

MF: And you were sitting around the Cabinet table at that time.

MC: Well, what I would say to you would be a couple of things. Take, for instance, a clear example, the food industry, because I know it very, very well, and they create €8 billion of exports for this country, and exports and trade is the way we're going to get out of this [...] situation we're presently in. [...] [W]hen you take [the issue of Sterling] out of where their bottom line is, it is then that you can see where the competitiveness issues are. But what are they? They are energy costs and we have worked hard with Eamon Ryan to reduce energy costs and will continue to do so.

We got onto the thorny subject of the property collapse. Again, Mary Coughlan's answer sought to stress what she felt had been achieved on the back of the boom, rather than accepting any culpability for the bust.

MF: Sitting around the Cabinet table when house prices were going through the roof and the builders were being treated like royalty [...], did you at any stage say, "God! We've a fierce dependence on this building industry. We've got to stop. This is getting unbalanced"?

MC: Well, I was thinking about this and the one thing that I'd have to say is, on the back of the boom, what did we do? What did we do with the money?

MF: What did you do?

MC: Let's [frame] it in household parlance, if you want. What we did was, we paid off our debt. In other words, in a house you pay off your mortgage. So that's what we did. We invested in that. The second thing was we invested in pensions. Any household would do likewise. As a consequence of that good political decision, we are now in a position to use those savings and invest them within the economy, given that we have such difficulties at the moment in accessing cash....

MF: Can I go back to the question?

MC: And the third thing is we provided new services. So, on the back of the investments, we made very, very good decisions.

MF: Are you saying to me that you don't think there was inordinate waste going on [during] those years?

MC: I would say there was an over-reliance on the construction industry and, as Minister for Enterprise, Trade and Employment, my view is that the way [...] we get out of this is [through] making very difficult decisions, public finance decisions, banking....

MF: But can I go back to the question?

MC: But investing in enterprise is where we're actually going to be.

MF: But can I go back to the question, because you were saying that, sitting around the Cabinet table, you're conscious of all the departments?

MC: Yes, we all would be.

MF: You all would be. Did nobody say, "This is madness!"? Did nobody say it?

MC: Yes. People said the price of land had gone through the roof. We had a lot of young people, young married people, single people wanting to get on the property ladder. That was a topic of conversation for a considerable period of time. People [were] perhaps over-exuberant in the way....

MF: Without a doubt!

MC: But we all were over-exuberant in our lifestyle. You had situations where we had very high employment [...].

MF: I know that! We all know that. And there is no doubt that we all colluded in it and we all congratulated ourselves on being the richest country in the world, which was a very dangerous thing to do. But, at Cabinet, where you're supposed to be running the country, did nobody say, "We have to stop this..."?

MC: Yes. We did. And we invested, as a consequence, in huge amounts of money in enterprise and in education, and in science and technology. And I just....

MF: No, but can we come back to the whole thing about the property bubble....

MC: Where we created opportunities for growth.

MF: The property bubble?

MC: Yes.

MF: You don't think the Government had any role whatsoever to play in stopping that?

MC: As I said, we were over-exuberant. Lots of people were over-exuberant....

MF: Including the Cabinet.

MC: But there was an underlying investment, at the time, because clearly, from an economic prospective, you cannot be over-reliant on one section of society or one section of income in order to survive [...].

I pushed her further on the issue of the great reluctance within the Government to take any responsibility for what had, and indeed was, happening.

MF: Bankers are blaming the world. Everybody's blaming [the] subprime [culture] and America. And nobody seems to be taking responsibility for the self-made problems. Home-grown problems.

MC: We had home-grown...we have home-grown problems. We just mentioned one of them, which is competitiveness. That is a home-grown problem and one which we certainly are working towards [rectifying]. Yes, there was an over-reliance on the construction industry. Nobody's taking from that. What we're saying is that, on the basis of our over-reliance on one or two industries, we spread ourselves too thinly. What criticisms we get is that, even with the monies that we did get, we didn't invest them wisely. I don't agree with that.

MF: Okay. Do you think the public finances are under control still?

MC: What I said was, we are managing and handling the public finances, and at this moment in time that's the process we're involved in. […]

MF: Do you think they're under control?

MC: What I'm saying is we're handling the public finances and we're making decisions that are prudent, appropriate and […] we have to get a balanced approach. […] We have to cut our expenditure again. We have to reduce those public finances and sustain them. We have to deal with our current and our capital spend, and we're also going to have to look at the issue of taxation, our tax base. Very serious issues, but let's look at the framework: we've a five-year plan. Everyone in the Oireachtas has agreed, and it was good to hear that every Opposition leader, plus the Taoiseach, has agreed, [to] this five-year framework. 2013 is the place to be and […] the end game is that we get back to sustainability.

MF: Why do you think there's a public perception that there is no leadership and that there are no decisions? That there is no plan? That [the people at the helm have] no confident plan, as it were? Because that is a perception.

MC: It is. Why is that perception there? One, we're losing a lot of jobs and people are losing their employment and that's very difficult for them, personally, and their families. And my job is to how to activate them, how to get them back into the workforce, or get them back into training or education. And that's very difficult for people, so they're going to say, "Well, how come I lost my job?" Then there's this public–private difficulty that you have between those in the public service and the private service.

MF: No, but I'm talking about the perception that the Government isn't tackling it.

MC: Well, I wouldn't agree with that. What has happened is, we haven't seen a situation [yet] where a number of issues have bottomed out. [For example], the banking issue is still ongoing. There isn't one solution, one answer. [...] So [things are at] that transient [stage]. We still have a lot of people losing their jobs. That makes people uncomfortable, frightened, concerned....

MF: Terrified!

MC: Terrified, some of them. So, we have all of these things that are shifting and moving and there hasn't been a stop [to them]. So, what we are saying is the five-year plan is a frame-work. These are the decisions [that] will have to be made. It has to be fair and balanced.

If evidence were needed of the "party before politics" allega-tion, Brian Cowen gave his enemies ample ammunition at the end of 2010. He travelled to Donegal for the November 2010 by-election the same week the International Monetary Fund came to Dublin to thrash out the first bailout, worth €85 billion. Many felt and voiced the opinion that his place was in Dublin behind his desk!

There had been widespread allegations of cronyism in Mary Coughlan's appointment and allegations that she and Brian Lenihan were in cahoots with Brian Cowen over his election as leader of Fianna Fáil and Taoiseach.

MF: Can I go back to the beginning of your appointment to your current position? You and Brian Lenihan nominated Brian Cowen?

MC: Yes.

MF: For leader of Fianna Fáil and, consequently, Taoiseach. How did all that develop behind the scenes?

MC: I'm trying to remember now. About this time last year, it was May, end of April, May. What happened was, the former Taoiseach Bertie [Ahern] indicated he was stepping down. We had to elect a new leader and the parliamentary party met. I got a phone call on a Friday morning from the now Taoiseach asking if I'd come in to see him. I met Brian Lenihan at the door in the Department of Finance, neither of us knowing why we were going to be invited in, assuming that Brian wanted to speak to everyone. And he asked us if we would nominate and second him. And it was a great honour to have been invited to do so and, within the parliamentary party, we were asked to put his name forward. And, as you know […], Noel Dempsey was asked in the Dáil to nominate him as Taoiseach and that was seconded by Dermot Ahern. So, that's how it happened. He asked both of us to come forward….

MF: And what kind of a conversation did you have that morning?

MC: Convivial enough…

MF: You're good mates with Brian Cowen, I gather.

MC: Well, first of all, I admire him. I've been in the Dáil with him – he was there before me; he was there in the time of my late father. He's a young man. We were both young TDs at the same time. I admire his acumen, his capability; he's a big party man. I'm big into the Fianna Fáil party. So, I suppose we have a lot of things in common. I worked very closely with him, particularly when I was Minister for Agriculture, because he was Minister for Finance....

MF: So what did you talk about that morning?

MC: We talked about where he was going to be, what his thoughts were about getting through the process of being the leader of the party; then would there be a competition, of course, for the leadership of the party. My considered view at the time was, because he is held in such high regard, that I didn't anticipate [any] competition, but that's not to say, as you know, Marian, that there's never any competition....

MF: And had you and Brian Lenihan discussed it?

MC: No, because neither of us knew the other was coming in the door in the first place. [...]

MF: And did [Brian Cowen] say to you at that stage that he'd be appointing you to the two senior ministries?

MC: No. No.

MF: It's kind of remarkable that two of the, as it were, not-so-senior ministers do the nomination and the next day they're Tánaiste and they're Minister for...

MC: Well, there was about a month in between in fairness…. I think it's important to say that we had a chat about the difficulties that were going to arise, what plan we had, what framework we have for the next number of years. Brian has always been in a position to ask everybody their opinion. He never shares that with anybody else. I remember [once] having to go in to see him before he was appointed Taoiseach and he said to me, "How many years are you in that Department of Agriculture?" And I told him and he said, "I think you might need a change. What would your interest be?" And I said I would like to get into something on the economic side….

MF: Why?

MC: Because I distinctly remember Mary O'Rourke saying […], "Women shouldn't always be put into the soft options." Now [that wasn't the case with my position] in Agriculture, since I was the first woman ever appointed to that [position]. You know, women were in Education, they were in Health and Social Welfare. Now, it's an honour no matter where you are, but I thought, "Right, I need another challenge." So, I thought an economic challenge would be appropriate.

MF: […] I don't mean this in any rude way, but what makes you think you're qualified for that role?

MC: Well, I've had twenty-two, twenty-three years of public life. I have been a minister for a considerable number of years. I work very hard….

MF: I have no doubt….

MC: I have a huge interest in the betterment of this country, creating opportunities for the generations that are coming behind [us]; […] I have two [children] of my own. My view of public life and public service is that the place you now find yourself [should be used] to provide a good legacy for the people coming after you. And that's where I have the interest and the focus.

In the general election in spring 2011, of the four party loyalists who were responsible for the election of Brian Cowen as Taoiseach, two – Noel Dempsey and Dermot Ahern – did not contest their seats (neither, incidentally, did Brian Cowen), and Mary Coughlan lost hers. All enjoy the benefits of a very comfortable pension. The fourth, Brian Lenihan, barely managed to hold on to his seat – he was elected on the fifth count. He was the only Dublin Fianna Fáil TD out of forty-seven returned to the Dáil, and has since died. Fianna Fáil is undoubtedly severely damaged, but it is far from a spent force. When it is returned to power, as it will inevitably be, it is unlikely to be the same political institution we all know so well. The era of the political dynasties is now over, surely?

5

Roy Keane, 01.05.2010

"I wouldn't be the most patient man on the planet..."

Roy Keane's name is synonymous with two things – world-class football[6] and absolute directness. Generally speaking, sporting superstars come across as one-dimensional, particularly football-ers. Increasingly, it seems as if their lives are managed by legions of PR handlers and personal assistants. The public events they attend and the charities they support are carefully picked (in the case of the latter, they are often to do with sick children), they smile for the camera, their wives and girlfriends are invariably glamorous, they drive ostentatious cars, they are paid ridiculous amounts of money, they say little and, by and large, their careers are over at age thirty-five. This is most definitely not the case with Roy Keane. He does not court the media, although his readiness to express forthright opinions means he is often in the spotlight. He seems genuinely surprised, but not the least bit upset, when one of those opinions proves unpopular with fans or the general public. Keane famously accused Irish football fans of hypocrisy over their calls to have the World Cup play-off with France in 2009 replayed due to Thierry Henry's blatant handball that saw France qualify at Ireland's expense. He railed against what he saw as sloppy defending on the part of the Irish team and pointed out, citing examples, when poor refereeing decisions had benefited Ireland.

Acutely aware of Keane's notoriously short fuse, I had intended to leave my home office an hour early on the day of my interview with him. As I was printing off my briefing notes I heard a beeping sound which reminded me of a notice from the ESB warning that our electricity would be switched off that day for a few hours. Luckily the printing was complete! I got to the gate in my car – we have electric gates – and the zapper didn't work. I was locked in! The keypad on the gate also refused to work. Back in the house, I couldn't find the manual key to release the gate. St Anthony was invoked but to no avail. Abject panic! At this point I thought I might have had a cardiac arrest.

A decent man called Steve came to the rescue. We drove across a field at the back of the house, across a stream and across another field (just about managing to clear a very boggy section) to a back gate. It was also… *locked*. There was nothing else for it. I rammed the fence with my car, with Steve doing all the "strong man" stuff. We got to another gate which was, thanks be to God, unlocked. I arrived with fifteen minutes to spare. The first question from Roy Keane's handlers was if I'd mind waiting half an hour, as Roy would like to have some soup and a sandwich… Certainly!

The interview with Roy Keane was due to take place in a hotel where he was attending an event for Guide Dogs for the Blind, a charity that he has supported for more than a decade. When we eventually sat down to do the interview, he struck me as modest and courteous. I asked him if he knew any other journalists who had rammed a fence to talk to him. He smiled politely. I suspected he hated this kind of thing, being interviewed, but I got the impression that, having decided to do so, he would just "get on with it". From the outset, he was disarmingly straightforward.

MF: How did you get involved with the charity?

RK: Well, the simple answer to that is I was asked. I was asked to get involved many years ago and, I have to say, I was a bit naive when I first got involved in it. I didn't know too much about the Guide Dogs, but […] I was interested. So, I got involved and, what, nine [or] ten years later I'm still involved, and I really enjoy it, I have to say, and it's opened my eyes, meeting volunteers […] [and] learning exactly what the Guide Dogs brings to people and to families.

So far so good!

MF: Talk to me a little bit about the difference between the thrill of playing [soccer] and what's required for management?

RK: Well, it's like chalk and cheese. Trust me. When you're a player, you just have to, in a sense, look after yourself, whether it be [as regards] preparation [or] going out and giving your all. When you're a manager, in a sense, you obviously have to trust the players a bit more. You have to do your preparation, but, I do believe, once [the players] cross that white line [...], [it's out of your] control. But when you're a player, you're out there, you can do something about it. And, going back to when I was eight, nine years of age, I always enjoyed that side of it. So, [regarding] the management, obviously I'm still learning. It's certainly more frustrating. At least, when you're a player, you can do something about it.

MF: I remember seeing you being interviewed before [...] some big Ireland match where there was lot of pressure on and the whole country had ground to a halt and all that, and somebody said to you, "Do you get nervous? I mean, how do you cope with the pressure?" And you said, "That's what I do. I love it."

RK: Yeah, I know. I was always comfortable with that side of it, I have to say. People talk about the big crowds. I'd probably get more nervous speaking in front of four or five people than I would ever [get] playing in front of sixty to seventy thousand, because I felt that's what I was born to do – play football. And particularly the position I was in: I was right in the middle of the park. So, I was always in the middle of the action and it never really bothered me whether there were fifty thousand people or five thousand. [...] I wouldn't say it was my job, but it was the love, it was something I always loved doing [...]. I loved everything about football and particularly the battles in the middle of the park. I always thought, particularly as I got older, I always thought of it as a massive battle and a bit of a war really.

MF: And you would be the warrior?

RK: Well, I enjoyed that part of it. I enjoyed the leadership that was brought on as I got older, particularly with the captaincy. I enjoyed leading the team out at the front of the tunnel – not that I was on an ego trip, but I was glad to be at the front and saying, kind of, "Let me at 'em!", you know. I never [got] involved. I never, sorry, enjoyed, as I said, the nonsense before the games, the media coverage before and after. I was saying just "Let the action begin!" Because there is a lot of nonsense written [...] about players and obviously the media intrusion [...] [has] gone [to] a level where it's pretty frightening. [...]

MF: But just to go back to when you were talking about the playing. You said it doesn't matter whether [there are] fifty or sixty or seventy thousand [people watching]. [There] must be an amazing adrenalin rush, all the same. Do you have a consciousness of it in some way?

RK: Well, I was always certainly relaxed before matches but, yeah, when you knew the referee was going to blow the whistle, or particularly when you're standing in the tunnel, [...] that's when I came alive. I felt I'd a kind of split personality. [...] I'd be driving my car to the ground and I'd get there – years ago – just an hour, an hour and a half, before the game. Whereas now you're in the hotel the night before, but years ago I'd get to the game at two o'clock, and I'd be dead relaxed, and I wouldn't come alive until about five to three, and I'd think, "Now, now the action starts." And I'd be, I think, this different person for an hour and a half [and] try and win the game and then go home and I felt, particularly as I was getting older and [...] when I got married and I had children, I felt like I'd a double life, and I'd go home and I'd try and be somebody completely different and I'd try not to bring my work home with me, or whatever it might have been, but come five to three or three o'clock, kick-off [time], I did feel like a different person. I have to say I just felt different.

MF: If you take being in management now […], I mean when you started at Sunderland, you [came] in at the top but you're also on a learning curve. Is that difficult? And also because you're so well known, every single solitary thing you do, every choice you make, every decision you make is going to be analysed and parsed backwards and forwards.

RK: But I think it's all part of when you're in a professional sport. But when I went to Sunderland, before I took the job – I'll be honest, when I stopped playing – I didn't have a clue what I was gonna do, which is not always a good thing, because you'd have to sometimes make some plans. But I'd been on a coaching course and I thought, "Yeah, I don't mind and I don't know if this is for me." And then the Sunderland job came up and, before you knew it, I was a manger. Things went reasonably well…but, as you said, when you do well, [you get] promoted and [you] stay up, and the expectation becomes hard, but I've always, I have to say, I've always been comfortable with that. […]

MF: Well, I suppose what I meant also was that you were on a learning curve and, while you were master of all you observed when you were playing, and you knew what you wanted to do and you knew how to do it, as a manager it's kind of different, isn't it? Because what you're trying to do is release other people's creativity.

RK: Possibly so and you obviously become a bit of a teacher yourself and you're trying to pass on whatever you think players might need. But the industry we're in — players are very funny, you know, they're all different — a lot of players might be on ego trips and I wouldn't have the...I wouldn't be the most patient man on the planet, because [I'm not patient] with myself, so I'm even going to be less patient with other people. So, that's something, I have to say, I'm trying to learn. And I think, to be a top manager, you do have to have certain management skills, which I probably lack at the moment, but I'll hopefully get there. But I still have my strengths. I still think I can become a good manager.... [...]

MF: And what kind of relationship do you have with the players?

RK: Em, I'm not really sure. [...] I think you'd be better off probably interviewing one of my players....

Towards the end of the interview, Roy Keane was characteristically frank when I pushed him a bit further on the subject of players and managers.

MF: Do you think that some of the young players would be intimidated by you?

RK: Intimated by me? Well, they shouldn't. They shouldn't really. For what?

MF: Well, because you have this image now of [being a] perfectionist, perfectionism and perhaps Puritanism, if you know what I mean.

RK: Well, I played under managers like that – Brian Clough and Alex Ferguson – and I loved it. I loved it. They were everything I dreamed of. They wanted improvement. They wanted players who trained hard every day, [who were] on time for training. I loved that environment. Players should enjoy that, and, as I say, you've got to obviously press the right buttons with certain players, but players shouldn't be... As I said, you'd probably have to ask the players who've played under me for a number of games. Listen, you'd always get one or two who are gonna be not happy [...] and I understand that. Listen, you don't have to love the manager, but you've got to have obviously an element of respect for him.

MF: Right. You're enjoying it, are you?

RK: Yeah. I do enjoy it – most of the time, yeah. It's...no, I do enjoy it, but it's obviously a hard job. That's why, as I said, unfortunately managers come and go very quickly.

Keane readily admits that he has a compulsive nature. He partied hard when he was younger and, on more than one occasion, got into trouble for it. He now has a reputation for self-discipline and high standards, but he has not forgotten his old wild days. But it was the shock of a serious injury that made him change his behaviour.

MF: When you say you make decisions kind of instantly.... [Y]ou got that terrible injury where you were out for nearly a year, wasn't it?

RK: Eight to nine months, yeah.

MF: And you had been on the tear, and you had been drinking, and you had been eating the wrong food, and all this stuff that you have mentioned yourself. And was it that, or was it when Ferguson picked you up when you were hauled in one night, into the clink, shall we say…? When did you say, "Listen, Roy Keane, you're gonna change tack here."

RK: Listen, I have to say, I don't think there was one incident where I said, "Listen, the penny's dropped for me here." But it was a number of things. […] [M]aybe I was taking my career for granted, and when I got the injury really I was in my prime, and it stopped me in my tracks. And I was a bit of a boy, listen, but I wouldn't change anything. I was a good one for going out and I never wanted a party to end. The usual carry-on. And then I'd a bit of bother when I got in a bit of trouble after celebrating – I think we'd won the League – and the manager came down and got me. So there was a number of things […]. You know, as I said, I don't think it was one morning I woke up and I said, "I'd better cop myself on!" I think it was a build up of lots of stuff, and when I got back playing [after the injury], I thought, "Listen, I want to play as long as I can and I need to kind of get a better lifestyle." So, it was combination of a number of things….

MF: Right.

RK: I basically stopped going out really, but I started spending more time at home, training properly, trying to look after my diet a bit more. But the strange thing was, when I started doing that, I probably went too far then the other way. I went too fit. My body fat went too low, and I still picked up injuries after that, because I lost too much weight. I went from one extreme to another. I went from going out a lot, you know, going missing for one or two days, coming back [at] all sorts of hours […] to becoming a fitness freak. […]

[A]t the time when I done my cruciate, my body fat would've been about 18 to 19 per cent — for a professional footballer that's too high. [...]

And, eventually, I think towards the end of my playing career, my body fat was probably four-point-something. So, I was too skinny. [...]

MF: Is that a kind of an all-or-nothing part of your mentality?

RK: Most definitely. Most definitely. And [...] that's not always a good thing. I think it helps me in certain parts of my life, but I'm trying to relax a little bit more now [...]. I don't think I'm as intense as I was. Because it tired me out. [...] I didn't even start slowing down. I just went from one extreme to another. I remember I went to a health farm in Milan when I was about twenty-eight or twenty-nine. I didn't eat for four days. It's like a detox place. I thought this would help me with my injuries, and I came back and my wife was going, "You're not even eating!" They gave me advice on cutting out red meat. So, I went from cutting out red meat to not eating any red meat. And I remember I was sick one time. I was off. I missed a game, and I was really bad. I couldn't even get out of bed, and I'd done some blood tests. My iron levels were down too low and the doctors said, "What are you eating?" And I said, "Well, I've cut out red meat." He said, "You must [eat meat]; you need that in your diet." But, the usual, I went too far the other way.

I am fairly sure that Keane either doesn't know or at least doesn't fully understand the scale of the turmoil, in Ireland and elsewhere, that he caused when he left the Irish squad during the 2002 World Cup in Japan, after a spat with Manager Mick McCarthy, a spat that became known as the "Saipan Incident".

The row with McCarthy concerned Keane's very public criticism of the facilities and the standard of preparation of the Irish team. We had a caller to the programme who told us that she rang her sister in India to check on her welfare – there was a real threat of war at the time between Pakistan and India – only to be told that Roy Keane was headline news there. It strikes me that Keane felt he was taking a principled position and he could not have cared less if the entire population of Ireland had begged him to return.

MF: How do you reflect on that Saipan thing now? Do you ever wish to God you'd stayed.

RK: No. No. I couldn't stay under the cloud that was there. Listen, I was no angel. I know that, but I was certainly frustrated. I think it was years of frustration building up to Saipan in terms of when we qualified, when we got there – and nobody will change my mind on it. Everyone has their opinions and everyone has shared their opinions and everyone's an expert, but there was nobody in that room when I was accused of faking injury, absolutely nobody, and that was [the reason] I was never going to go back. [...] [W]hen I came back, they were saying I [...] would I go back and play, but players, I felt, should have supported me. I know what I would have done if it was one of my team mates. So, some people show their true colours and that's not me. [...] I couldn't have played in that World Cup, not after [what] went on. If when I went to Saipan, could I have been a bit more patient and tolerant? But people weren't there. They didn't see our training facilities. We keep talking about organisation at top level sport. We talk about the Irish mentality and it was the same old scenario: "This'll do us." And I'd had enough of it, I have to say. I'd had enough. […]

MF: I suppose it was the timing.…

RK: The timing was everything. I suppose people say, "on the eve of the World Cup", but if ever it was going to happen, it was probably going to be, you know, on the eve of the World Cup. It was never going to happen before a friendly match, but I'd years and years of [banging my] head [against] a brick wall, and if people criticise me, then.… Listen, we're all different. I like to try and do things properly, not to perfection, but try and make progress. I'd stated my concerns to everybody, the manger, the players, and we went over there and there was this meeting and, ironically, we'd got over the hurdles of me being upset with the set-up and disagreements and we were flying out the next morning. So, everything had been taken care of and then certain people brought up certain stuff and accusations of me faking injury which, if anything, it was me playing through injuries that made me finish at thirty-four years of age. Ask the other players. They're playing till they're […] thirty-seven, thirty-eight. I finished only because I played through injuries. It was the other way around. So, people throw that at me, and even now, to this day. I wouldn't accept it off nobody. Absolutely no chance.

MF: Had you any sense of how big this was at home?

RK: Not really, because, again, we were in Saipan and I was rooming on my own and, when it all came to a head, I was in my room […]. No, […] I felt and I still feel it was the right decision. […] [L]isten, again, when I went to the World Cup, I wanted to go there with Ireland, try and give us our best chance. I knew [...] everything wouldn't have gone smoothly. Far from it.

MF: Yeah, but, we were in with a chance...

RK: Of course.

MF: In that particular year.

RK: Of course we were. Yeah. I couldn't agree more with you, but I never got to experience that. I'd done my bit. We'd qualified. There'd been hassles in the build-up. We'd no training pitch. Now, people can sit in their studios. People can sit at home. We'd no training pitch. We'd no training gear. Why bring us all the way to Saipan if we haven't got that stuff? Now, people say to me, "It was supposed to be a relaxing trip. People playing golf." That is not my idea of preparing for the World Cup and I cannot argue all day with people who say, "Ah, well, you know, you've got to chill out somewhere." I appreciate that. We could have chilled out in the afternoon, but if we were going to train — train!

Two players got injured in the first two, three days. One player fell down a pot hole, which seems to have been forgotten about. A pot hole in the middle of the training ground! We couldn't believe our eyes. What we'd seen when we walked out there! But some players, and I wouldn't be critical of them, some players were like, "Well, this is the way we do things." But I'd had enough of it. I'd been involved [in Irish soccer] from going [...] up to Dublin as a fifteen-year-old. I mean, [I was] told I was too small. So, I'd years of saying, "Listen, what is going on here?" And I bit me tongue. You know, don't worry, I wasn't ranting and raving all the time, but it came to a head and I thought, "I'm the captain." And we talk about the Irish fans spending fortunes.

At least give them an opportunity for us to have the best chance of getting through the group....

So, I have to say, [I have] no regrets about the World Cup. I wish, in a sense, it didn't happen, because we would have prepared properly and given ourselves a better chance. But, again, it's unfortunate [...] that people, and even now, like to second guess: "Oh, you should have done this...". And they haven't got a clue what went on.

It is refreshing to meet somebody with so little regard for the opinions of others, which is not the same as saying Roy Keane is uncaring. Clearly, his family provides an important anchor for him, although he readily admits that he is not one for extended periods of time around the home with his wife and children. He is proud of the normality of his life: "My life is very simple. If I'm not at work, I'm at home watching television with my children, going on school runs, walking my dogs or going to the pictures. That is my life in a nutshell and I have to say I think it disappoints people." He is happy that his only son has only a passing interest in football.

MF: Your young son is eleven now, is he?

RK: Aidan, yeah. I've only got one son.

MF: Is the love of the game coming through, the talent?

RK: No. No. He's got more interest in, unfortunately, all this PlayStation stuff. And no. He has very little interest in football.

MF: Really?

RK: And, to be honest, yeah, I'm not too upset with it. You know, he's got his own [interests], [and] I don't put pressure on [him] to focus on any sport. The school he goes to, he plays all sorts of sports and [he has a] kick around, don't get me wrong. But, he's not on any team. He doesn't really watch many games with me, or if I do go to a game, sometimes I have to drag him with me, but other than that he's got his own kind of little life to lead.

MF: Right. Because, when you were eleven you knew [playing football was] what you wanted.

RK: Oh, most definitely! I was eight or nine years of age when [...] I thought, "Listen, I want to be a footballer."

MF: Right. Well, maybe one is enough in the family?

RK: Possibly so. As I said, people automatically think, because I've been involved, obviously, I've got four daughters as well, but with my boy, no. Good luck to him. He does what he wants, and he's a good young fella, so whatever decisions he'll make will have very little to do with me.

Maybe Keane's very mature attitude to his son is informed, to some extent, by his intimate knowledge of the life of a Premiership footballer. He gave a very telling insight into the reality of life for the retired footballer when I asked him about his friendship with some of those he had played with during the glory years.

MF: Are you friendly with any of the folk [...] you played with?

RK: Em, like who? Who?

MF: Well, I'm just wondering [about] the team, you know [...].

RK: I'd say hello to people if I met them, but I wouldn't....

MF: You wouldn't be meeting them.

RK: No, it doesn't work that way. I played with players at club level for twelve, thirteen years – good lads – and if I saw them tomorrow, I'd have good craic with them. I'd say there's two or three players I've kept in touch with throughout my career. That's just the way [...] football is. I roomed with Denis Irwin for years with [Manchester] United and Ireland, and me and Denis don't speak to each other, but if we see each other, we say hello. So, it's nothing personal.

MF: I thought you were still friendly with Paul McGrath. I don't know where I got that.

RK: No. I spoke to Paul a few months ago. I got his number. Yeah. Paul, now, I'd pick up the phone to Paul and maybe Nicky Butt [...]. There's three or four I'd keep in touch with, but players are funny like that. It's a funny kind of industry where everyone kind of moves on, you know. That's where it's a bit cold, football, like that.

In his autobiography, Keane says he believed he wasn't a dazzler, that his talent and success had more to do with slogging. Well, he slogged and he dazzled, and he was and is enormously respected for it.

6

Nuala O'Faolain, 12.04.2008

"The goodness went out of life…"

Nuala O'Faolain rang me in March 2008 to arrange a lunch – we were good friends and had a running gag about birthday lunches, which could be had in any month of the year or in many months of the year. We met on the following Monday in a busy restaurant in Dublin. She came in using a walking stick and dragging her leg a bit. Other than that, she looked terrific. Presuming she had sprained her ankle, I asked her what had happened. Her reply, in its directness, was classic Nuala: "I'm dying. I have cancer in my lungs, tumours in my brain, probably elsewhere too. It has metastasised. I will take radiation but not chemotherapy." Bam. I felt disbelief, horror. And a great desire that this was some awful, awful mistake. It took several minutes to sink in.

I first met Nuala O'Faolain when she was a contributor to RTÉ's *Women Today* – a programme about convent education. This must have been in the mid-1970s. Unusually, the programme was pre-recorded in the producer's apartment so we had some time before and after the interview to get to know each other. Nuala was brilliant on that programme — it was the first time I experienced at first hand her unique blend of articulacy and hilarity. Of the many letters we received afterwards, one man wrote saying how we had nearly caused him to crash his car into a tree due to the tears of laughter streaming down his face. We became close friends and occasional colleagues – both of us worked on RTÉ's *The Women's Programme*. She also did a stint as literary editor for *Status*, a magazine I was editing; Nell McCafferty was another contributor.

There is always a tendency to speak of one's friends in glowing terms, especially when they have died, but Nuala really was a one-off: fiercely intelligent, opinionated, articulate to an astonishing degree, erudite, but also loyal, vulnerable and, despite being prone to melancholy, great, great fun. She was no saint, either, and could drive you nuts betimes! She could boss for Ireland and in an argument you had to hold your own fairly fiercely. But those arguments and disputations were great, great fun as well.

At that lunch in 2008 we discussed the necessity of truth around dying and how there should be no lies; no claiming false hope, which often only serves to isolate the dying person even further. Talking about death and dying, and the pain and fear of it, was not new territory for us. Nuala was godmother to my daughter Sinéad who died in 1990. But Lord was it hard — shocking — to be having that conversation again, knowing for sure that yet again the outcome was 100 per cent certain.

We (unbelievably, in retrospect) discussed in a relatively matter-of-fact fashion the idea of doing an interview. Nuala really wanted to do it. I was still reeling from the news, still trying to absorb the enormity of what I had just heard. We must have looked strange to the other diners that day — to the very jolly party further down the restaurant — locked in an intense discussion, both of us in tears.

Since Nuala became a successful author in the late 1990s — her memoir *Are You Somebody?* had become an international bestseller — I had interviewed her on a number of occasions. It became obvious to me that, for Nuala, being interviewed live provided her with an important means of understanding herself. It was as if answering questions under pressure marshalled all of her considerable gifts, allowing her to speak with her wonderful blend of candour, wit and passion. I had seen these same skills in social situations, particularly when she was locked in an argument with somebody. Every part of her positively glowed with concentration; her arguments flowed in full, perfectly formed, reference-laden sentences.

After our lunch, I called Anne Farrell, my producer of many years, to get her opinion about the interview. She was, obviously, deeply shocked by the news but on balance felt that we should proceed. The interview with Nuala was pre-recorded in Galway. We picked Galway because that's where Nuala was having the radiotherapy and we planned to do the interview in the hotel room where I was staying. By that time, Nuala had lost her hair and was very bloated from the drugs, but there was nothing wrong with her brain.

It turned out that the recording equipment I had taken with me was faulty, so I called the RTÉ studio in Galway to explain the situation. At one point I found myself practically inside a wardrobe as I tried, as discreetly as possible, to explain I was interviewing Nuala O'Faolain, who was dying. How ridiculous in retrospect, considering we were about to embark on a conversation of brutal honesty. But the studio was a good move; it provided a useful distance between us. We held it together. She was magnificent.

On the way back from Galway after the interview, I called Anne Farrell to say I wasn't sure if we could air the programme – after all, it was hardly the usual kind of material encountered on mainstream radio on a Saturday morning. And what about all the other thousands of people who were dying from or being treated for cancer? We got together the next day and listened to it together – Anne knew it was an incredible interview but both of us were really worried that the content could seriously upset some people. We discussed the various issues for days. Eventually, we agreed that it should be aired but only with an explicit warning at the front. This was the first time in my life as a broadcaster that I found myself actually advising listeners to turn off their radios. Anne organised for the psychologist Tony Bates, who had hospice experience, to listen to the interview and to participate in the programme to deal with any issues. And the Irish Cancer Society set up a special helpline to deal with any distressed callers.

Listening again to the interview and reading the transcript I am struck by Nuala's articulacy – the interview was completely unedited. Some of the interview was conducted through tears – on both sides – but her wonderfully truthful command of language never falters, not even for a second. With most interviewees, I tend to begin with a few more general questions to put the subject at their ease. But this was different. There was nothing for it but to start, to "just do it" as Nuala was so, so fond of advising others to do.

MF: When were you diagnosed?

NO'F: About six weeks ago. I was in New York. I have a terrific life, to be absolutely honest with you. I managed to buy a little room that I absolutely loved and the important thing about the room was that it was mine, because for several years myself and this man I liked were trying to pretend that I was part of his family, him and his 14-year-old daughter, who lived in a house in Brooklyn. I had at last managed to negotiate that I wasn't ever going to be any good of a stepmother, that she didn't need me, that she had a good mother and a good father. I didn't need her; that I didn't want to spend my life watching her doing her homework. So I gradually semi-moved out and I used to go to music and meet my friends and eat, and I was writing a book, and I'd applied for a fellowship to write a book, and, of course, I had Ireland. So everything was well.

But I was walking along one day after fitness class and my right side began to drag, and I eventually went to A&E in a New York hospital, a thing I wouldn't wish anyone to do.

MF: Why?

NO'F: Because it is full of chaos and people who have been shot and run over and [...] − I couldn't get over this − I spent thirteen hours on a little gurney and the two people beside me were there for unhappiness. [...]

Anyway, I was sitting there waiting to hear what was wrong with my right leg, when the guy came past and said, "Your

CAT scan shows that you have two brain tumours and we're going to do X-rays to see where they're from; they're not primaries." And that is the first ever I knew.

MF: He said that in the middle of A&E?

N.O'F: Yeah. He just passed by and I was on my own, you know. He just passed by and a few hours later he passed by again and said, "Oh, the X-rays show you have lung tumours", and since then, of course, others turned up. So that was New York six weeks ago and since then I stayed a few nights in hospital. I might mention a bill of $28,000, but I had some health insurance through my dear friend John. But I sort of knew that I should come back to Ireland and I was absolutely right.

MF: How did you deal with the information?

NO'F: I couldn't deal with it…I was so shocked I would pay attention to anything except what I had just been told. And it took me a long time to work my way a little bit out of shock.

In Ireland we tend to think that we do death and dying very well, and certainly the tradition of wakes and large funerals are a wonderful way of helping those who are grieving. But we often put, it seems to me, intolerable pressure on the person who is dying – to make it easier for those around them – to participate in the great deception that everything will be alright, when it is sometimes patently obvious that it will not be. I asked Nuala about her prognosis and the possibility of treatment. Her frankness is almost too difficult to take in.

NO'F: There is no chance of a cure. There's a chance of aggressive treatment that will gain you time, often good time. And I came back to Ireland and did fourteen brain radiations, and the idea was that I would move on to chemotherapy [...].

The question arrived. I was supposed to start chemotherapy. I was supposed to start eighteen weeks of it, six goes of it. After three goes they would know if it was working.

But whether it was the disease or the brain radiation, I don't know or care, [it] reduced me to such feelings of impotence and wretchedness and sourness with life...and fear...that I decided against it.

I pushed her on her rejection of treatment and how people in similar situations to her might find little of hope in her words.

MF: Very often you hear people being told, "Oh, you have got to have a positive attitude" and "a positive attitude is what gets you through" and I have betimes thought that this put a lot of pressure on the person that was told to have the positive attitude. What's your own view on that?

NO'F: Yeah, I was just reading about some best-selling man who says, "Live your dream to the end" and so on, and I don't despise anything anyone does, but I don't see it that way. Even if I gained time through the chemotherapy, it isn't time I want. Because, as soon as I knew that I was going to die soon, the goodness went out of life.

MF: I think that's a very interesting thing. Because, as I understood it, for you, life was very sweet: you had sorted out your American life, you had your life in Ireland, you had your life in universities, and then you were going to write.

So life was very sweet for you at that point. Why does it not seem that if you went through treatment that it could be sweet again?

NO'F: It's the time that I would get at the end of the treatment. I'm not even thinking about the treatment itself. It amazed me, Marian, how quickly life turned black, immediately almost.

For example, I lived somewhere beautiful, but it means nothing to me anymore — the beauty. And, for example, twice in my life I have read the whole of Proust. I know it sounds pretentious, but it's not a bit. It's like a huge soap opera. [But] I tried again the week before last and it was gone; all the magic was gone from it.

And I'm not nice or anything — I'm not getting nicer. I'm sour and difficult, you know. I don't know how my friends and family are putting up with me, though they are, heroically. And that is one of the things you learn. [...]

MF: If there are people who have cancer or loved ones who have cancer and passionately believe that the treatments are going to work for them, there is the possibility that this could cast a despair over them.

NO'F: My despair is my own; their hope is their own. Their spirituality is their own. My way of looking at the world is my own. We each end up differently, facing this common fate. I wish everybody out there a miracle cure.

Every single professional will tell you that they cannot say how long it will be…and it is my choice not to go the route of chemotherapy. Funnily enough, I don't care about losing the hair. What I do care about is that sometimes I see people frightened or repulsed, and that is why I went and got a wig in which I look like a rather striking but elderly chorus girl.

Now I am beginning to put the auld bald head out there and I still have a few eyebrows, but what do I want them for? I don't care about anything any more. I know everyone says the hair matters, but that is not true. You can put a little cap on or something for the hair. That is irrelevant compared with having to leave the world behind.

MF: You said it wasn't so much you leaving the world as the world leaving you.

NO'F: I thought there would be me and the world, but the world turned its back on me, the world said to me, "That's enough of you now, and what's more we're not going to give you any little treats at the end."

MF: Like…

NO'F: Like, let's say, adoring nature. Music is not quite gone, but I'm afraid it will go if I overdo it. So I'm trying to listen to as little as possible.

One of the reasons I went to New York was to hear live music, which I did the night before last – a wonderful string quartet – and thanks be to God my heart responded because if I had had to sit there listening to Schubert's quartet *Death and the Maiden* [and it] meaning nothing to me, I really think I would have thought, "I am going to throw myself under the subway train" […]. I came out elated. There are things left.

I still occasionally like food and above all I like sleep, and what I am hoping for, and I don't think this is going to happen, but if I could have this – I kinda hoped there was some kind of way of fading away, that you lay on your bed and you were really a nice person, and everyone came and said goodbye and wept, and you wept and you meant it, and you weren't in any pain or discomfort, and that you didn't choke and didn't die in a mess of diarrhoea, and you just got weaker [...].

[My cancer] is already in my liver and I don't know what that means, but if that means that sometime in the middle of the night, on your own, as you must be, you know you are just about to go into the dark, [then] that's what I want. [Crying]

Nuala was very interesting on the subject of God and the possibility of an afterlife.

MF: Do you believe in an afterlife?

NO'F: No, I do not.

MF: Or a God?

NO'F: Well, that's a different matter somehow, you know. I actually don't know how we all get away with our unthinkingness. Often last thing at night I walked the dog down the lane and [I looked] up at the sky illuminated by the moon and behind the moon the Milky Way [...]. And you know you are nothing on the edge of one planet compared to this universe unimaginably vast up there, and unimaginably mysterious.

And I have done that for years, looked up at it and kind of given it a wink and thought, "I don't know what's going on." And I still don't know what's going on, but I can't be consoled by mention of God. I can't.

MF: Would you like it?

NO'F: No. Oh no, I wouldn't. If I start doing that then some-thing really bad is happening to my brain, because though I was baptised and I remember my First Communion, and I went to all Catholic schools, and I was in the legion of Mary, and I tried to stick to my pledge; and though I respect and adore the art that arises from the love of God, and though nearly everybody I love and respect they [...] believe in God, it is meaningless to me, really meaningless.

MF: The reason I asked you was because I think it is a source of comfort for many people.

NO'F: Well, I wish them every comfort, but it is not even bothering me. I don't even think about it. I have never believed in the Christian version of the individual creator... I mean, how could I? I know far too many Buddhists and atheists and every kind of thing.

Let poor human beings believe what they want, but to me it's meaningless. I waited the other night to listen to the radio [...] to hear poor John O'Donohue, knowing that he is very important to many people, but, to me...I just gaped. It's beautiful to him, but it is utterly meaningless to someone it isn't meaningful to.

And yet I want to mention one thing that you might play at the end. I know you don't play records, particularly for dying people, but still. [...] There's a song I heard a few years ago that everyone else knows except me and it's called "Thois i Lar an Glanna"– it's a kind of modern song, 1929 I believe, and it's sung by Albert Fry and I think other Donegal singers. And the last two lines [...] [ask] God up there in the heavens, even though you don't believe in him, to send you back yesterday, even though you know it can't happen. Those two things sum up where I am now. [Crying]

Nuala's attitude to the afterlife and to God rankled a few people. I certainly had comments from people after her church funeral, either saying that she was disingenuous in her interview or implying that she had had a deathbed conversion. Nuala had no such conversion – the contradiction, if there is one, is that she believed passionately in ritual which provides a ready means for cultures to deal with important events. In the week before she died, she planned all of her own arrangements. She wanted a Roman Catholic church funeral, despite offers of a secular service. More particularly, she wanted to be buried alongside her beloved brother Dermot (Dido). She decided on the inscription for her tombstone; she sorted out her will. The mass was celebrated by Professor Fr Enda McDonagh, for whom she had great respect. When her body was being taken from the church the whole congregation joined in "Sé mo Laoch mo Ghile Mear". That would have given her great pleasure.

It was obvious from the extraordinary response to the programme that Nuala's words gave an enormous freedom to people who are frightened of dying. Even in her absolute despair she was eloquent and was capable of putting her own particular circumstances in perspective.

NO'F: Well, I am sick, but I am trying to say goodbye. So much has happened and it seems such a waste of creation that, with each death, all that knowledge dies. [...]

I think there's some wonderful rule of life that means that we do not consider our own mortality. I know we seem to, and remember "Man, thou art but dust", but I don't believe we do. I think there is an absolute difference between knowing that you are likely to die, let's say within the next year, and not knowing when you are going to die – an absolute difference.

MF: So people don't kind of move away from you? Or how do people deal with you, I mean friends. […] Do they crowd you out?

NO'F: Obviously sometimes. In fact, often, I pray for them to go away, for the very essence of this experience is aloneness and, anyway, I think it is the steroids keep you awake at night. So it is two in the morning or four in the morning and you're walking around – but you're not walking around; you're staggering around – and all you know is that whatever it is you are feeling or thinking is yours and nobody else's. And there is nobody to lay it off on, and that aloneness is the centre and the thing that you never know when you are well….

MF: And […] because everybody has to go through this, essentially on their own.

NO'F: And those are the two things that keep me from the worst of self-pity […]: that, first of all, everyone's done it, so that ordinary people are as brave as I could ever be or as less brave as I could ever be. Everyone's done it.

The second thing that really matters to me is that, in my time, which is mostly the twentieth century, people have died horribly, billions of people have died horribly; when I think of people dying in Auschwitz or dying in Darfur, or dying of starvation or dying multiply raped in the Eastern Congo […], I think, "Look how comfortably I am dying. I have friends and family. I am in this wonderful country. I have money. There is nothing much wrong with me except dying."

When I think of how privileged I am. And I had two brothers who died of drink and they died miserably and underprivileged and here I am, as usual, the lucky one in the family. [Crying]

The reaction to the programme astonished everyone, particularly Nuala. We had hundreds and hundreds of letters and emails responding with compassion to her visceral and utterly unsentimental words. Many came from cancer sufferers. One woman in particular comes to mind – she was terminally ill. She and her husband heard the introduction to the show and he turned off the radio and left the room. She turned it back on and wrote to say how endlessly helpful it was to hear all of her own emotions, fears and loneliness expressed so honestly. It allowed her to be more open with everyone from that point – a liberation for her and for them.

The response gave Nuala a great lift – again and again she talked about how she had not realised there was so much goodness in people. After the reaction to the interview, she told me that she wanted very much to do a second interview. "To redress the imbalance" were the words she used. But it was not to be – she died a month after we did the interview. True to her word, she continued to say goodbye to the world, including going on a trip to Berlin to look at art and hear music, and going with her family to Sicily.

Listening back to the interview now, three years later, I can hear the stress in her voice, her determination, her unflinching attitude to terrible truths. I regret we did not get to do the second interview.

7

Christian Pauls, 20.06.2009

"Make yourself knowledgeable, please..."

It's often said that Queen Elizabeth II is the perfect diplomat because, in almost six decades on the throne, she has never once expressed a personal view. Nobody knows what she thinks about her Prime Minister, the UK's membership of the EU, the loss of the British Empire, her own family's occasional dysfunction...For this reason, interviewing diplomats can be a less than rewarding; mostly all you get is one bland platitude after another. They tend to be briefed beforehand. The diplomatic life is a strange one; it is nomadic, hard on partners and children, and largely organised around formal gatherings where protocols dictate everything.

Christian Pauls, the former German ambassador to Ireland, doesn't do bland – he tells it as he sees it or else he sees no point in talking. All hell broke loose when he was reported to have given voice to some uncomfortable truths about the Irish in a speech in Clontarf to a group of German business people in 2007. Gay Mitchell MEP, who had been at the gathering, had taken particular offence and subsequently called for his removal. Knowing that the Ambassador was due to retire in 2009, we made a direct approach to get him on the show, since we felt that going through "normal diplomatic channels" might not succeed. It worked. It's the kind of approach he understands and respects – I think he would not mind me referring to him as a maverick diplomat! Pauls is a serious, very straightforward, straight-talking man. But it takes very little for his devilish sense of humour and gentle irony to emerge.

MF: Tell me about being an ambassador. How would you define the role? What's life like for you? What do you want to do representing your country, and what do they want from you?

CP: Well, it depends on the country where you serve, so let's talk about Ireland because that's the closest. If you look at relations between Ireland and Germany it would be very difficult to find anything we disagree on, so the political work is certainly not to the fore in my work. If it is political work, most of it relates to European issues and are mainly dealt with in Brussels, or even between capitals directly, not through the embassies. So, you're a spokesperson for your own country, as I am for Germany in Ireland. I like to address people and it's not always in very critical terms, I can assure you, and [...] talk about Germany and try to convey my picture, or the picture I have of my own country to various groups – students, at schools, universities, people in business, etc. I guess most of the work we do as an embassy is legal and consular work, which nobody sees but which is very important, and then press and cultural work.

It became obvious, as the interview developed, that there was nothing glib whatsoever about the Ambassador's willingness to express his views. He was born in the dying days of World War II, September 1944, and his father was a senior officer in the German army. The experience of being born in post-war Germany had a deep effect on him as, indeed, it had on his entire generation. I asked him about his father's attitude to his own involvement in the war.

MF: Your father was quite senior within the army, though he was very young?

CP: Yes. He was a General Staff Lieutenant Colonel and I guess at the end he was the number one Staff Officer of the German Division fighting in the West.

MF: And I gather that you think that, by being in the army, you could distance yourself a bit from the politics.

CP: Well, that's a sort of meaning he gave to me and I have heard this from various other older men who probably, in 1933 or so, or 1934, when Hitler had taken over, thought that the army would be more-or-less a non-political entity, even under the Nazis. Well, they soon found out that they were completely wrong about it.

MF: And did he talk to you much about it as you were growing up?

CP: No. He never spoke about the war with me. I guess the first time he did that was when I was doing my military service and was a twenty-year-old or nineteen-year-old.

MF: And how did he reflect back on it?

CP: Well, I guess most of it was with horror. He'd been on the Eastern Front; [he] lost his left arm on the first day of that campaign. Then he had been in Italy and later on in the West, and I guess all of these men who came back out of the war, looking back at it, said, "How did we ever get into this?"

Even more remarkably, Pauls senior was appointed as Germany's first ambassador to Israel.

MF: What is particularly remarkable, in my view, is that, roll on the years, and your father was the first person appointed as German ambassador to Israel, which must have required a certain view of him by Israel and a certain view of him by the authorities in Germany at that stage?

CP: On the German side, I believe, although I don't know this, they would probably have said, "Okay, so he was one of twelve million soldiers in World War II? He's taken up another line of work. He is working for us now, so why shouldn't he qualify for any posting we have for him?" From the Israeli side, I mean there were huge demonstrations against him. It was certainly known that he had been in the German army and very many people didn't want to see a German ambassador there at that time, and they certainly didn't want to see a German ambassador who had been a soldier and a highly decorated soldier. But it still was possible in 1965. I believe if it had been 1975 or 1980 it wouldn't have been possible anymore because the Israeli society had become so much more aware of the Holocaust or *Shoah*, as they refer to it. And probably in those early years, fifties and sixties, they really had enough to do to build up their own country, and perhaps they were also [turning] a bit away from the remembrance of all this horror. But ten years later I don't think he would ever have been appointed ambassador.

MF: When you think about the date, 1965, the very fact that anyone would have been sent as an ambassador from Germany was pretty remarkable. It's amazing how things move on, isn't it?

CP: Oh yes. Well, there was lots of work which had gone into that. The first talks between Israelis and the German side, they date back to the early fifties. There was always the question of was there anything we could attempt to [do to] at least atone a little bit for our crimes. It was a highly sensitive issue with the victims first of all, less so for the perpetrators.

MF: And I gather that stones were regularly thrown at [your father's] car.

CP: When he handed over his credential, it was the car of the Israeli President. So it wasn't German government property; it was Israeli government property.

MF: Because the Israelis protected him?

CP: Oh yes. I remember the first six months [he had] something like six bodyguards around the clock.

99

The tongue-in-cheek speech that caused offence to Gay Mitchell and others related to some of the more unseemly behaviour of the Irish during the affluence of the Celtic Tiger years. Pauls' speech, delivered to a largely German audience, took issue with, among other things, Irish doctors who refused to work in the public service for a salary of €200,000, traffic congestion and immigration. During the interview he mentioned that his own daughter, a 39-year-old paediatrician working as the deputy head of one of the largest child clinics in Berlin, earns €90,000. He also retold a joke to illustrate the Irish obsession with money, privilege and status. At the National Concert Hall one evening a loudspeaker announcement requested that the owner of a 1993-registered car move it as it was blocking an entrance. Nobody came forward... because nobody wanted to admit that they were not driving a new car! It was reported that Dermot Gallagher, the secretary general of the Department of Foreign Affairs, had a terse exchange with the Ambassador, leaving him in no doubt that his views were "inaccurate, misinformed and inappropriate at a public forum". Pauls came in for further criticism in 2009 when he made remarks at an event in Tralee, Co. Kerry warning of the consequences of a second rejection of the Lisbon Treaty by the Irish.

MF: When you made your remarks in Kerry about Ireland and Lisbon, because I gather you're very passionate about it, you got rapped over the knuckles from home?

CP: Yes.

MF: And what did they say to you?

CP: To shut up. I wasn't being helpful.

MF: And what did you say to them?

CP: Well, I did shut up. Remember we were supposed to have a meeting a few days later which didn't take place? Well, they thought I was entering a domestic debate.

MF: What did you say [in Kerry], or are you allowed say what you said?

CP: Oh, yes, certainly…

MF: Because I can say what you said if you can't say what you said.

CP: No. I said if…we look at Lisbon II, the second referendum – which the Taoiseach has now addressed yesterday – I said you will be deciding Ireland's future with this. This is not just repeating the first referendum where everybody really didn't probably know to what length the vote would be weighing on everybody's shoulders later on. And I said that everybody is going to know what [Lisbon II] is all about.

MF: What did you say in Kerry that got you into trouble?

CP: Well, basically, [it was implied that] I had been threatening the Irish electorate. I certainly advised them in very strong terms to vote "Yes", but what was not reported was that I was speaking a lot more about solidarity among Europeans and Kerry than I was talking about Lisbon II. But, it was picked up by *The Kerryman*, which I presume was not very friendly towards Lisbon I, and so it was a bit slanted, the report.

There were calls for Pauls to be sent back to Germany following the incident in Kerry.

I pressed him on the unique position of the Irish electorate in being able to vote on Lisbon. His answer was eloquent and straightforward in the way that it referenced his early years in post-World War II Germany, when the European project was first mooted.

MF: There is a sneaking suspicion here among a substantial number of people [...], possibly even a majority of those who voted the last time, that if the people of Germany and the people of France and the people of the Netherlands, [...] if the British got a chance to vote, that they'd all vote "No".

CP: Well, that might be the case. Certainly the Dutch and the French have expressed views on voting which were Euro critical. I was really offended by remarks being made from the "No" side that Ireland was the only real democratic country in the Union because there the people were asked to vote on this and all others were denied the right to vote. This is unspeakable arrogance. We have another system. There is almost no element of plebiscite or referendum in our system – on the level of the states which make up our federation, yes, but not on a national level. And there are some very, very good reasons for this. I don't think I need to remind fellow Europeans of how Germans voted in referenda in the 1920s and 1930s, and how they were caught by various political sides [...]. I believe the founding mothers and fathers of the Federal Republic were a bit suspicious of the wisdom of the people after our own experience and said, "No. We have representative democracy and we believe it will work for us better than something else had worked for us." So, please, when talking about our system, take a look at our history. And we believe we made the right decision. And stop telling us we are not democrats.

Christian Pauls was particularly frank about the inherited guilt his generation of Germans feel acutely: "It's a topic which is foremost in our mind, has always been and will be until we die…".

I had encountered this firsthand myself. Years ago, I went on a walking holiday, the sort where you walk from hilltop town to hilltop town and your luggage goes ahead of you. The group of us, all strangers at the outset, were made up of Swiss, French, English, Dutch, Irish and German people. We met in a restaurant on the first evening without guides, a "getting to know you" evening when everyone was tentative, polite and friendly. We became close to the German couple over the course of the week – she was in her late forties and he in his fifties. The first-night meeting on holidays like this sets the tone, with everyone anxious to maintain a pleasant camaraderie. To my astonishment, and after a bewildering short space of time, the German woman was in tears and desperately trying to explain that she had not been born until after the war and so was not responsible. I was sitting directly across from her. At the risk of sounding like that gag from *Fawlty Towers*, nobody had, as far as I could tell, even mentioned the war.

Dealing with Germany's history is something Christian Pauls still finds inexplicable and bewildering. But that is not to say that he has no views on how this particularly awful period might be better understood. One of the callers to the show asked a very simple question, "How do you explain it to kids? My son is seven and into history, but I dread the day he asks me about the Holocaust."

CP: I don't know how to explain it. I had the same question with my four daughters. I think we told them at the beginning these were the facts, instead of trying to explain something which I am unable to explain – I mean, I was even unable to explain it to myself. Why did it happen? How could it happen? There are very good books written for children, too, on this issue. I remember one is *When Hitler Stole the Pink Rabbit* by a Miss Kerr, who was the daughter of a famous German theatre critic in the 1920s, [where she writes] about her youth in Nazi Berlin. That's probably the best way to get children to look at this phase of history.

MF: To give them the books and then you can discuss it afterwards?

CP: I would tell them, before giving them the books, "This is a book on a period of German history which you should know about." Then I would tell them that we murdered millions – six million Jews and more – simply because they were of another faith, race, what will you, and [I'd say] the war that we unleashed, in total, cost fifty million lives. I think one should be able to bring these facts to the attention, let's say, of a ten-year-old and if they follow a bit, or if they listen to parents talking about this or that catastrophe in today's world, whether you look at Afghanistan or Iraq or Pakistan… So I don't think it's that far out for them simply to grasp it, but then give them a good book which […] approaches them at the level of a child.

Pauls is a very serious man. His refreshing frankness is no more than an expression of his extreme thoughtfulness. And, of course, the rather unflattering portrait he painted of Ireland and the Irish during the boom years seems, in retrospect, rather benign!

8

Ross Hamilton, 01.09.2007

"God's sick sense of humour..."

The reputation of and respect for the Catholic Church in Ireland has taken such a battering over the past two decades that it is sometimes difficult to appreciate how all-pervasive its authority once was. The full scale of the abuse of generations of children by members of the clergy, and the repeated attempts by the Church authorities to cover the scandal up, is still unfolding. In retrospect, the indiscretions, if I might call them that, of a few individual clerics appear relatively benign.

Fr Michael Cleary and Phyllis Hamilton, his housekeeper, were the parents of Ross Hamilton, who grew up with his mother and father in Fr Cleary's house in Ballyfermot in Dublin in the 1980s and early 1990s. The couple had had an earlier son who had been given up for adoption.

I had direct experience of Fr Cleary when I worked on religious programming for RTÉ. In the lead-up to one of the abortion referendums we took the decision to host one big debate – Church versus State – close to the date of the vote, when all the arguments would have been well and truly thrashed out. We gave ourselves good lead time in which to invite the senior representatives of all churches. All but the Catholic Church agreed to participate relatively quickly, but the Catholic Church did not refuse. Each time we made contact we were told that they would let us know. On the day before the recording we still didn't know.

On the morning of recording we were told that Fr Michael Cleary would be their representative. This was acutely embarrassing. The other church leaders had accepted our invitation in good faith and on the understanding that each church would be represented by a senior figure. And we now had Fr Michael Cleary! The other church leaders were understandably furious. I thought that one leader would, in fact, not take part.

I introduced Cleary as "a bishop for the purposes of the programme", since it was the Catholic bishops who had nominated him. We had asked for an archbishop or at the very least a senior bishop. Immediately he started with old guff about just being ordinary, simple, one of the lads, etc., and joked about his lowly status. This was cringe-inducing for me and the other programme makers, and ignited fury in the other guests. Even now, years later, I find the level of duplicity between Cleary's carefully cultivated public persona and image and the reality of his private life staggering, almost impossible to understand.

We did the programme. Afterwards, the other church leaders complained. I know they thought we had been disrespectful to them and their churches. We apologised profusely. The Catholic

Church of that time clearly did not respect the dignity of the other church leaders. This would be unimaginable now.

From day one, Ross Hamilton was a secret. Fr Cleary, a champion of the poor, liked to give the impression that he was open-minded and liberal enough to employ a single mother under his roof. At various points in Ross's early years he began to sense that his household was not like others. "Don't call him 'Dad', call him 'Father'" – clever that! Then, when he was ten years old, he was let in on the secret. He *was* the secret.

My first impressions of Ross were of a pleasant, perhaps diffident young man. Warm and though understandably nervous, he was very forthcoming. He was sometimes movingly honest in answering hurtful questions about his bizarre and destructive upbringing. Time and again throughout the interview I was touched at his extraordinary lack of bitterness and blame, and his genuine sense of humour about the strange circumstances of his upbringing.

> MF: Did you know about you? […] And I ask that question because I think that if you're born into a situation, no matter how great it is or how awful it is, up to a certain age you think, "This is the norm."

> RH: That's your reality. And that's the only one you know or remember.

> MF: So when did you twig that the way you were living was perhaps a little bit different to everybody else?

> RH: I think I was about four, three or four, and I was outside the house in Ballyfermot one morning and my best

friend at the time, Alan Plummer, I was telling him […], I don't know, something like "Mummy and Daddy are up in bed together." And he's like, "Priests can't get married." And that's one of my earliest recollections because I remember, well, I wasn't sure what "married" meant at that stage anyway, but […] I kinda twigged there was something wrong. I can even go back to that moment and see the spot I was staring at. Then, over the years, just little by little it kind of dawned on me, and I think I was more than willing to ignore it as I realised there was a problem there that they didn't want to tell me.

MF: And then the crunch came when you were about ten, because you had created this fantasy for yourself of a really flash dad, so to speak.

RH: Yeah. I was in school and […] if one kid's dad had a Ferrari or a Beamer or something my dad had two….

MF: Standard enough.

RH: Until eventually someone went, "You're full of crap", you know, and I kind of realised just exactly how full of crap I was. And then I went home that night and I asked my mother [who my father was] and she sat me on her knee and she kinda looked at me and she said, "Guess." And I went through a wish list of fathers, you know, and then eventually she kind of gave me this look and I just said, "Father?" and she went, "Yeah." And then she started crying; I started crying – I really didn't want him to be my father at that stage. I think, whatever he felt about me, I was quite embarrassed that I might grow up to look like he did. You know, the big beard, no teeth, big belly, floppy bald-hair. I think it was my hair I was most worried about.

Fr Cleary was a big noise in the Catholic Church in Ireland in the 1970s and 1980s. He was a natural showman and became one of the Church's most charismatic campaigners during the divisive abortion and divorce referendums, when the direct authority of the Church was being seriously challenged. On social and moral issues he was an arch conservative. He waxed lyrical about family values and the evils of contraception. He was passionately opposed to abortion and asserted, disingenuously, that all feminists were pro-abortion. He was also opposed to divorce, believing marriage to be the cornerstone of society and Christian teaching. Fr Cleary was adept at exploiting a variety of platforms from which to air his views. As a priest he regularly preached from the pulpit to a captive audience. He made numerous television appearances where he presented himself as "a gas man", a man of God, a man of the people. But he also worked as a broadcaster in his own right, hosting his own radio programme, which he used to take issue, unchallenged I might add, with anyone who disagreed with him. For a time, he became known as "The Singing Priest", after he released two albums of music. Ross was aware of his father's charisma and how it often led to behaviour that made him sail very close to the wind.

MF: But yet, in his own way [your father] was kind of like a superstar. He adored the limelight, didn't he?

RH: Yeah. He was a natural performer, I think is the thing. [He loved being] the centre of attention and, yeah, he adored the limelight. But he used it for a lot of good in his life. Looking back, there was a certain amount of lunacy in what he was doing, you know.

MF: Yeah and the other thing about it is he invited [...] – he had some nerve – he invited a film crew...

RH: To come and live with us.

MF: To come and live with you! Even though there was this big, dark secret.

RH: That's one of the big questions – why did he do that? Or was he setting it up for later? I dunno.

MF: And presumably your mother was scared witless, too?

RH: [...] Looking back, I didn't realise how scared [...]. I've seen some of the footage now and she hated being filmed. But, yeah, she probably thought he was absolutely bonkers to be letting them in.

Ross was particularly insightful on how his father managed the day-to-day hypocrisy. Interestingly, Ross never actually used the word "hypocrisy", preferring instead to refer to his father's situation as "disingenuous" or "deceptive".

RH: I think he put himself in a situation where he had to represent the Church. So if he veered from what they told him to say or what their stance on things was, he got in trouble and he moved down the ladder rather than up the ladder, but at the same time [...] I think he would have believed a lot of it. I mean the abortion thing: he would've really believed in the sanctity of the foetus at whatever stage, once conception has taken place. And, once a person believes in that, the way people like that do, [...] it makes perfect sense that what you're doing is murder. [...]

MF: He said one thing but he did another. [...]

RH: He was playing a game of cards with God in his head, I think, and he thought that at the end of the day he'd win. Him and God [would sit] down at the table, they'd work it all out and everything would balance, the books would balance.

MF: Do you think that's what he thought?

RH: I think that's what he thought. He was taking his chances and he was never caught while he was alive.

MF: So he got away with it.

RH: Yeah, but he didn't. I mean, the last moment I saw him wasn't a nice romantic cinematic goodbye between father and son. A bunch of us were brought in and he was in the throes of dying. He was on morphine – really bad – and he just wanted his watch on his hand and stuff [...]. He wanted his watch, and to me that says he wanted more time and maybe he was thinking, "Jesus, I should make this right before I die." But at that stage it was out of his hands. It was too late.

Although I knew several priests and senior clergy who thought Fr Cleary was a bit of a buffoon and a bully, the Church hierarchy seemed to have approved of him, at least in his professional life. He often dismissed theologians who expressed a different point of view from his on, say, the relationship between Church and State with, "Ah you know these theologians can do too much thinking and reading...I am just a simple priest who preaches the Christian message." So I was surprised to hear from Ross that, in fact, he had read extensively. Not a crime after all!

One of the more surreal, almost unbelievable, aspects of the entire affair was how Bishop Eamon Casey had, in Ross's words, "read the riot act" to his father – Casey had become aware, apparently, that Ross and his older brother were Cleary's children. Casey himself fathered a son in 1974, a fact that did not become public until 1992. The confrontation with Casey provided an opportunity for Cleary and Ross to at least attempt to clear the air between them.

MF: Is it true that Bishop Casey had bawled [your father] out? Bishop Casey knew, didn't he?

RH: Apparently so. [He knew about] both my older brother and me. He'd apparently read him the riot act. I've heard mixed stories from one of my aunts, but basically he read him the riot act and apparently he never told my dad that he had a son.

MF: Strange times! I mean, nowadays […] probably anybody under the age of twenty-five would say […], "There you go! It happens." But […] at the time it was an enormous scandal. But you did get to a point, did you not, of being father and son?

RH: Yeah. Once we were in that situation we had to have the sit-down and it was very uncomfortable. I really would have preferred to go on with the façade.

MF: Really?

RH: Yeah. It was just really uncomfortable and I suppose for it to happen at that point felt a little bit disingenuous as well, you know, that it was just out of fear that…

MF: That you were discussing it.

RH: That we were having this confrontation, yeah.

MF: And was it a confrontation or was it a discussion?

RH: It was a discussion. There was no argument. It wasn't a big row. It was more of a solidarity kind of meeting, but there was a confrontational element to it, you know. There was, "Let's finally confront this."

MF: What did he say to you?

RH: […] [He] just said, "Ross you know that I know that you know" [laughs]. And I was like, "Oh, God! Can I not just eat my breakfast and get on with things?" And then we talked it out and the fact that we would have to be careful who we talked to and it was all like a solidarity meeting. And then there was a group family hug, but it wasn't…it was very uncomfortable. I found it very uncomfortable.

MF: Did you feel you were being denied?

RH: I think … little by little I was realising, you know, exactly how denied I was. […] [I]t's weird unless you grow up in it, you know what I mean? You've already accepted so much. […] [P]lus I didn't want the trouble or the hassle. […]

MF: Did your mother and he have rows about the hypocrisy of the situation, because at that time there were a lot of

113

priests […] who said they were having relationships with women, left [the priesthood] and got married?

RH: I know. There was one friend of the family who did actually leave the priesthood and got married. I dunno. It could've been his biggest moment, actually, if he'd confronted the issue […]. I don't know. After he died I started reading all sorts of stuff – spirituality, theology, philosophy, psychology – loads of books he had in his office. He'd everything from the Hindu religion to what-ever, and it just seemed to me that no matter what spiritual or theological background you're in, the truth is meant to be first and foremost. It's meant to be paramount, second to nothing and so, I dunno, […] it seems kind of absurd for him to lead that deceptive life. But, then again, […] he told my mother he didn't have what the priests call "a calling" […]. They're supposed to have some kind of calling and he said it was just like a natural career move almost. He never had a calling.

MF: Really?

RH: Yeah. That's what my mum said anyway.

MF: Because his public face was – now, I know you figure that the Church in some ways used him – but his public figure was very doctrinaire and particularly on matters to do with sexual relationships.

RH: Yeah. It's kind of funny that way, isn't it? I think he was pushed into dealing with these situations, which is kind of, you know, God's sick sense of humour, I guess. But he was the most experienced in these matters, I guess [laughs]. […]

MF: I presume you were at [your dad's] funeral?

RH: Yeah.

MF: Were you up in the front?

RH: Near the front.

MF: And your mum?

RH: We had to argue a little to make sure — [...] it was the only time I kinda put my bib in to make sure that my mum was in one of the cars, that we were in one of cars, because [...] it would have looked strange if we didn't, if we weren't there, because everyone knew that we lived in the house and everyone knew we were at least close anyway. So if we weren't there it would have looked like we were trying to hide something and I just thought it would've been heartbreaking for my mum to be just, you know, stuck somewhere in the middle, or the back. So there were a few little tentative moments, but we were there. [...]

MF: And, again, I remember hearing your aunt [Fr Cleary's sister] saying, "Absolutely not. No way. Under no circumstances. No way, no way, no way!" — that you were not his son. Was that very hurtful for you? [...]

RH: I was expecting it. I was in on it [...] from [an] early age so I was kinda expecting that. [...] It was agreed that we were gonna keep it secret so I would have expected that. The fact that they got so passionate about it was a little bit hurtful, I suppose. Adamant, or whatever.

MF: You seem very un-bitter about it all.

RH: Well, if I was bitter I'd probably be sitting somewhere on a park bench with a bottle of whiskey right now. I nearly went that way.

Three weeks after Fr Cleary died of throat cancer in 1993 *The Phoenix* broke the story that he was Ross's father. Cleary's sisters continued to deny that there was any truth to the allegation. After the funeral, the Church authorities closed ranks.

RH: After my father died, there were a few priests that knew us...And they came around and they were sympathetic and tried to be helpful, but immediately there were lines drawn...I think that was not through their fault but through the higher-up guys. It was just a case of finding out what we intended to do and, you know, trying to manipulate us, I suppose, and it was all very business-like – apart from the few friends of the family that were priests.[...]

MF: You know, I'm just thinking about things like Christian values and all that.

RH: Yeah! They didn't seem to feature all that heavily. I think, once money's involved and once the PR of the Church is involved, it's not very Christian.

It's fair to say that Ross and his mother's experience, in terms of how the Church treated them after his father died, was not all that different to that of clerical sex abuse victims. The Church took minimal action, hoping they would go away quietly.

MF: And did he make proper provision for you after he died?

RH: Yes, he was supposed to have had. Yes and no. We were supposed to be sent to see someone – I won't mention them for legal reasons or whatever in case we get in trouble – who was supposed to have some funds for us and help us manage them and set up a new life. To this day, those funds never appeared and it was implied to me by the person in question that they were there and then they changed their mind. I've since heard [...] other accounts backing up that the money should have been there, so it still kind of makes me angry when I think about it. [...] [W]e were kind of left stuck.

MF: And there were bills to be paid. And presumably Phyllis had no income of her own, other than as a housekeeper.

RH: No. No income.

MF: So, what happened? You were living in the house which was owned, I presume...

RH: By the Church.

MF: By the Church. What happened there?

RH: The Church provided us with a lawyer and we sat around for a year while the lawyer placated us and stuff until we eventually knew that nothing was happening. They were just going to leave us there until we got bored and went away or something. I don't know what they were thinking of doing, but our local doctor, our GP, he had a friend who was a solicitor and he took us on and things started moving. We were really in the situation where, [...] to secure money and to have people stop pointing the finger at us, [we decided] to just come out and tell the story. So he went looking for the best deal he could get us and we went with the *Sunday World*, Paul Williams.

Cleary's sisters continued to deny that Ross was their nephew and he was forced to have a DNA test to prove paternity. At around the same time, information about Cleary's older son, Doug, also became public. Ross dropped out of school and descended into a spiral of self-destructive behaviour – hardly surprising, maybe, given the extraordinary lie he had been forced to live. Added to this, he sometimes encountered a certain frostiness in people, as if he was being blamed for the fall from grace of his father.

> MF: I get the feeling that [you] not only [had] personal diffi-
> culties but you feel that the rest of the country resented you
> saying who you were?
>
> RH: Yeah. Yeah. There's definitely that feeling and I think
> there are some people who still have that old attitude, like
> they still find me a bit of a freak or something. Subcon-
> sciously. They wouldn't be rude to me – consciously rude to
> me – but […] some people have a standoffishness and you
> can tell that they just, I dunno…
>
> MF: Blame you?
>
> RH: Well, not blame me but see me as, I dunno, the black
> sheep […]. [It's] just a feeling you get sometimes, but it's
> getting less and less as the years go by.

By far the most moving part of this very affecting interview for me was when I asked Ross about religion. His reply is one of the most wonderful testaments to the ability of the human spirit not to be broken, not to be poisoned by bitterness and resentment. And it's hard not to read, in his reply, a salutary reminder to the Catholic Church of how its unChristian abuse of power and privilege damaged the lives of so many.

MF: Are you a believer?

RH: Ahh, I was dreading this question. Yeah, but what I believe is a lot simpler than what a Roman Catholic would believe. I believe in the Christian philosophy. I believe it was good that it was written down and that people followed it. I think Western civilisation kinda sprouted up from it and people the world over have gotten better in some ways because of it. But, then, a little bit of truth can be quite dangerous and then people can use it to manipulate the masses and stuff, and that's the worst thing, because then if people discover that that's been done to them, why should they believe in anything? […]

Ross Hamilton and his mother were, in a serious and destructive way, sacrificial lambs to one man's ambitious career and ego. After he died, they continued to be excoriated and denied for what was his "sin". How Ross Hamilton has survived as a pleasant young man with remarkably little tendency towards recrimination is nothing short of a miracle. His mother and father should be very proud of him.

9

Pamela Izevbekhai, 22.11.2008

"I had become an outcast..."

Of all the interviews in the book, this is the one I keep turning over and over in my head. I still find it completely bewildering – after all, I spent an hour or so with this woman alone in the studio, looking into her eyes, as she recounted with great emotion the story which captured the attention of the entire country.

By the time I interviewed Pamela Izevbekhai in November 2008 her fight for asylum in Ireland for her and her two daughters had already received a significant amount of coverage in the press. It was, on the face of it, a harrowing story of a mother who had gone to extraordinary lengths to safeguard the welfare of her children. Her very human story did, however, throw a number of national and, indeed, international issues into stark relief, not least of which were Ireland's asylum policy, the practice of female genital mutilation (FGM) in parts of Africa and

Nigeria's desire to downplay the incidences of FGM to protect its international reputation.

Pamela Izevbekhai claimed that she had travelled to Ireland in January 2005 from Nigeria via Holland with her two daughters, using forged passports. Later that year, when Deportation Orders were issued, Pamela disappeared and her two daughters, Naomi and Jemima, were taken into care by the Health Service Executive (HSE). From her hiding place, Pamela pleaded with the then Minister for Justice Michael McDowell to reject her deportation on humanitarian grounds. She claimed that her eldest child, Elizabeth, who had been born in 1994, had bled to death as a result of FGM and that her other two daughters could well be subjected to the same barbaric practice if she returned. Pamela was eventually captured and imprisoned for a month in Mountjoy Prison, at which point her case became a *cause célèbre*.

The woman who arrived in the studio to be interviewed was good looking, well dressed and possessed a good mastery of English. I had seen photographs of her daughters and they were gorgeous. Appearances should not matter one single iota in any case, but, of course, they do. Pamela came from a well-off family with houses, cars and staff. Some of Pamela's supporters pointed out that anyone who would voluntarily stay in an accommodation centre for asylum seekers in Sligo for up to six years, far away from her own home, husband and culture, clearly required asylum. Let's face it, the "creature comforts" at home, in Pamela's case, were way better than what any asylum seeker gets here in Ireland.

I asked Pamela to explain her family background because this had a direct bearing on the situation as she outlined it.

MF: Tell us a little bit about who you are and where you came from.

PI: […] My name is Pamela Izevbekhai. I take great pride in my name. I'm a simple person, you know. I'm a Nigerian, obviously, and [was] schooled, born, bred in Nigeria.

MF: And you were educated by Irish sisters, I understand?

PI: Yes. I was educated by Irish nuns at a private school, [a] primary private school.

MF: And after that?

PI: I went on to secondary school and started working and met my husband and got married.

MF: You didn't come from a very poor family, sure you didn't?

PI: No, I didn't.

MF: And are your own family still alive − your parents or your siblings?

PI: Well, unfortunately, I lost my dad very recently, but I still have my mum. I have one sister and I have brothers.

MF: And are you conscious within your family of which tribe you belong to?

PI: Yoruba.

MF: Is that an important part of your identity?

PI: Yes it is.

MF: Is it more important than the Nigerian?

PI: First of all I'm Yoruba and then I'm Nigerian.

MF: I don't think Irish people understand that. Can you explain why, what that means?

PI: Well, there are several ethnic groups that make up Nigeria. And we have a lot of different beliefs – cultural beliefs, traditional beliefs – and ways of doing things in each ethnic group. We have a lot of similar traditions, but we also have particular differences....

Pamela told me about how she met and married her husband Tony. He was from a different ethnic group to her – Edo – and they had a son Adrian who, she claimed, was about to turn eighteen at that time. It was not until the birth of their second child, Elizabeth, in 1994 that, according to Pamela, the differences in their ethnic backgrounds began to manifest themselves.

MF: Tell us what happened after that.

PI: I'll just tell you as it is. At the hospital after I had Elizabeth, my in-laws said to me – because what happened with Adrian was, at the hospital you had to get the doctor to circumcise the child before taking him home – [...] I was asked when I wanted to circumcise Elizabeth and it sounded very funny. I said, "She's a girl!" But my in-laws said, "Yes. She's a girl but she has to be circumcised." I thought, "What are you circumcising?" And I was looked at in askance as if, "Don't you know?" But my mother-in-law left me at that point, you know, and she just walked out and I found out later that she just went to the doctor to ask for arrangements for the child's circumcision and she was promptly refused. The doctor said, "No. I don't circumcise female children." Anyway, I didn't get to know that until much later. Then we went home. She didn't broach the subject anymore.

We got home and we were making preparations for Elizabeth's naming ceremony where the family gather, and pray and call, you know, depending on your tradition [...]. And we were preparing for all of that and my mother-in-law said to me, "Look, we have to make arrangements for the child's circumcision." And I said, "I don't understand what you're talking about 'circumcision'. She's a girl. Why would you want to circumcise a girl? What are you circumcising?" And she told me that they have to cut off the clitoris and I was mad. I said, "No! That's not happening to my child!" And she said, "Well, sorry, you don't have a choice in that." And I said, "What do you mean I don't have a choice in that?" [A]nd she went on to say…to teach me about their culture and I said, "But why didn't you tell me this before?" And she said, "Well, I didn't imagine that you wouldn't know, because it's supposed to be a natural thing, a normal thing. Why would you be walking around with your clitoris?" And it just baffled me, you know, and I just said to her I wasn't going to discuss it anymore with her and I waited for my husband to come back and I asked him. I said, "What is all this about circumcision?" And he said, "What circumcision?" And I told him, I relayed everything that had gone on between myself and my mother-in-law and he then said he was going to look into it. He didn't understand it himself. He'd never heard of it. He knew about male circumcision – and this is where, you know, the foreskin, the skin that is folding on the male genitals, is removed for health reasons – but he didn't know about female circumcision.

Anyway, we had a long and hard battle trying to avoid it and it became a big issue. It became a family matter. It became something that estranged me from my in-laws because I was looked on as somebody who didn't want the betterment of their child. [...] [They said,] "[...] [Y]ou don't have a say in what happens to these children. They are Izevbekhai children. Therefore, we tell you what to do. You don't know what to do. You have come into our culture so you have to learn." And because I was refusing I was gone against in so many ways. It went on and on, and one day my husband just came back and said, "Listen. I think we just have to do this for Elizabeth, not because it's what I want but just to bring peace", because it was too stressful. He couldn't relate with his family properly. He was caught in between. I had become an outcast at this stage [...] and I guess the man was just stressed. He was young, too, and he didn't know how to handle it. I didn't know how to handle it. And he said, "Let's just obey them because it's like we're disobeying them." I just said, "Is that what you want? Is this what is important to you?" And he said, "Well, it is important." And the next morning I just got my stuff. I took a small bag and put a few things in it and I called my helper at home then and I said to her, "Please, look after my children for me." During the night I didn't sleep [...].

Having fled the family home for four days, Pamela went on to describe how, under intense pressure from her in-laws and fearing that her marriage would fall apart, she agreed to and was present at the FGM of Elizabeth, who was seventeen months old at the time.

MF: So, did you give Elizabeth to your mother-in-law or what happened?

PI: Well, yes, I had to…At the end of the day I let them carry out the mutilation on her, but the tradition is that you are there sitting. So, after Elizabeth was circumcised, as they call it … it's not circumcision, it's cutting of the clitoris….

MF: It's mutilation.

PI: Yes. They gave the child back to me and gave me an ointment to use on her.

MF: And were you there?

PI: Yes.

MF: And did the child scream?

PI: The child was screaming. The child was in agony. I mean being brutalised like that…there was no anaesthesia applied. The child was just spread apart and held and she was shrieking. She wasn't screaming; she was shrieking. Her voice, it just went to my brain and I, at that point, I knew I'd done something wrong and then I thought, "Oh my God! I should have just run away with this child." I knew I had made a mistake.

At this point in the interview, Pamela used her hands to describe what had happened. There were tears in her eyes.

MF: And did you take her to hospital then?

PI: I did but she had bled too much. They kept telling me, "Look, calm down!" because I kept saying, "This child is bleeding." And I could see she was pale. She was…she was changing…her hands were getting cold [and] she was shivering […]. [B]y the time we got to the hospital it was too late for her because she'd lost too much blood and the doctor was really annoyed with me. He was really…he just…he just looked at me in amazement – couldn't believe that, you know….

MF: That you allowed it to happen.

PI: Yes. And he tried and tried…. [Crying]

Pamela claimed that she had intended to have no more children and that her marriage suffered as a result of Elizabeth's death. However, two other daughters were born and, although her husband had promised he would never allow either to be subjected to FGM, her in-laws applied intense pressure which often ended in violence towards her husband, to the point that her life became intolerable. Pamela was forced to monitor her children's movements at all times because of the constant threat of abduction. She claimed that they were forced to move house on three separate occasions.

MF: So when did you decide to run away?

PI: My husband was told that [his family was] going to have a meeting and the meeting was to clear up what was happening. But somebody who's very, very close to my husband and who knew what was going to happen just told my husband, "Look, if you love your wife and you love your children, you will get them out of here. They're not coming here to have any stupid meeting." My husband then said, "Okay. Fine." And he tried his best, looked for ways and means for us to get out, and he said, "You have to leave Nigeria now, because I don't know where I'll keep you."

MF: And he paid somebody to take you.

PI: Yes, he arranged...he made all the arrangements himself.

MF: And you and he are in contact all the time.

PI: We are.

MF: [...] Can he come and visit you here?

PI: Well, if he's given a visa, he will come.

MF: I guess that's unlikely, given your circumstances?

PI: Yes.

Pamela Izevbekhai got wonderful support from many people, including people in Sligo who befriended her and her daughters. They minded her children. She even got a civic reception in Sligo City Hall. She met with senators and TDs at a packed meeting in Leinster House. She got support from Amnesty International in relation to FGM. Famous names like Mary Robinson, Roddy Doyle and Mary O'Rourke spoke publicly in support of her case.

As most people are aware, Irish officials, including a Garda detective inspector, visited Nigeria in May 2009 to verify Pamela's story as part of her legal battle – more than twenty-five appearances in the High Court and Supreme Court alone, and ultimately an action to the European Court of Human Rights – to stay in Ireland. They could find no record of Elizabeth's birth or death certificate, no evidence of medical treatment or, indeed, her burial. The eldest son she claimed she had abandoned in Nigeria with her husband was, it transpired, her stepson. The documents Pamela had produced in her battle for asylum appeared to be forgeries.

Several other facts came to light. In 2004 Pamela Izevbekhai was issued with a UK two-year "family visitor" visa, casting doubts on her claim that she came directly to Ireland via Amsterdam. The immigration service has suggested that she did not apply for asylum in the UK (to which she could freely travel between 2004 and 2006) because her husband's visa would be automatically revoked, risking his ability to manage business interests he had there. Her original Deportation Order was in 2005. She is now back home in Nigeria, having been deported with her daughters on 18 July 2011.

There is no doubt that FGM is a widespread practice throughout many parts of Africa – the World Health Organisation estimates that more than ninety million women over the age of nine have been subjected to this absolutely barbaric practice, and as many as three million girls are at risk each year. Where laws exist prohibiting the practice they are often poorly enforced, fines and penalties are minimal, and prosecution is virtually impossible when the parents are complicit.

During the interview with Pamela an official from the Nigerian Embassy in Dublin, Onochie Amobi, came on the line. He was at pains to point out that FGM was not tolerated by the Nigerian Government, although he conceded that if the parents supported the practice there was little that the law could do. In any case, FGM is not specifically banned in Nigeria at a federal level, although some individual states have outlawed it. Prosecutions, where they occur, tend to be via human rights legislation rather than laws specific to FGM. Mr Amobi pointed out that a law specifically banning FGM had been passed in Edo State in 1999, Pamela's husband's home state. In July 2011 the European Court of Human Rights ruled that her family was well-off and could afford to protect the children.

All of this information only emerged after the interview was broadcast. The calls to the programme that morning were largely in support of Pamela's asylum application, many citing the plight of her two children, though there were those who were seriously opposed to her and her daughters staying in Ireland. Had she concocted or enhanced her story because the threat of FGM is very real in Nigeria? Some studies say that at least 23 per cent of women have undergone some version of the mutilation, and in certain areas it's as high as 65 per cent.

What does the case of Pamela Izevbekhai tell us about Ireland and our attitudes? Why did this particular case get so much attention and credibility? Maybe it is one of the great strengths of the Irish — that ability to see beyond the niceties of rules and laws and respond to a very human story. Having spoken to some of the people who supported Pamela, I've some across a wide spectrum of views. More than one close friend of Pamela's believes every word she said. Forged documents, they pointed out, were to be expected. Others felt deeply let down; others disillusioned. And others still feel hostility towards those who helped her. Was Pamela as manipulative as her many detractors believe? Taking into account coverage of people seeking asylum elsewhere (the US for example), there is a belief among asylum seekers that ticking the required boxes is not enough, that you have to ratchet up your story to improve your chances and this can include making false claims. There is, allegedly, a mini-industry in coaching people on how to maximise their chances. If I was in same position would I not lie to spare my daughters from this barbaric practice, even if there was the remotest chance of it being carried out on them?

Now that Pamela is back in Nigeria, presumably those she accused, her husband's family in particular, do not think highly of her. One friend who is still in touch with her told me that she is trying to avoid attention, that she does not feel safe. At the time of writing, she declined to speak to me, but she is still in contact with her Irish supporters. Maybe the truth will never emerge.

10

Martin Donnellan, 03.01.2009

"You want to treat people with a bit of dignity..."

A few years ago I went to the funeral of a retired chief superintendent of the Gardaí. The church was packed with Gardaí of all ranks, including the Commissioner. From the altar, one of the deceased man's sons mentioned that his mother always took the view that her husband had been just living with her – he was married to the force. A ripple of assent was audible from the congregation.

I worked on RTÉ's *Crimeline* for eight years in the 1990s and had seen firsthand the *esprit de corps* of the Gardaí. Former Assistant Garda Commissioner Martin Donnellan, then a senior officer and a regular on the show, was one of the best exponents of this shared sense of loyalty and pride. He is a natural storyteller and often, after the programme, he would have us in stitches by regaling us with stories, many of which came from Connemara where he had worked for a time.

Donnellan agreed to be interviewed on radio after he had taken an unsuccessful court case against the Gardaí because of his forced retirement at the age of sixty. I was intrigued to talk to a man who many regarded as the living embodiment of the Gardaí about why and how he had taken his employer of four decades to court. He had had an enormously successful career with the Gardaí and had clearly enjoyed every minute of it; he shared many stories during the interview of his time in the Gardaí and the cases he had worked on. What had compelled him, the seemingly perfect "company man", to sue his employer?

MF: But for you to take on the [Garda] Commissioner, the Minister [for Justice, Equality and Law Reform] and all that, it was to step out of a character that you have fulfilled all your life.

MD: It was really, to be honest; and, you know, some smart guy said, "Oh, God, Donnellan's a rebel now. He's, you know, all of a sudden he's developed into this rebel that we didn't know was there." But [...] that was not the intention of the action. I mean, I'm a company man. I have never, ever been disciplined in my whole forty years [of service] for anything, and I'd be a team player, really, you know....

MF: And were you embarrassed about that?

MD: I was a bit, but not really, [at] the end of day.

MF: Did they slag you over it?

MD: No. No, they didn't. No. No. I had a retirement "do" and the Commissioner came and made a presentation and colleagues, about four hundred [of] them, all came. Now, that did lift me out of the gloom that I was in, in the aftermath of the case, you know. But it is a lonely place. It is a lonely place. I have to say that.

A change in the rules relating to the retirement age of certain ranks in the Gardaí[7] had come about in the wake of the Imelda Riney murder case,[8] when aspects of the Garda investigation were criticised for lack of coordination. Changing the age of retirement down to sixty was designed to ensure that younger members of the force were promoted. As is so often the case when an individual takes a principled stand, Donnellan had many supporters, although most of these disappeared once his case had been unsuccessful.

MD: As it got nearer the court case it got more stressful, and in the aftermath I had lots of people wishing I'd win it, and they had obviously [a] vested interest. They felt that, superintendents and chief superintendents felt that, if assistant commissioners got [later retirement] that they had a good chance of getting it. They had been negotiating with the Department since 1990 about getting parity with assistant commissioners and commissioners [...] in terms of age [...] and assistant commissioners from 1951 had the right to work till sixty-five [...]. So they were fighting it on the basis that they wanted to get parity. They wanted to get to sixty-three maybe or maybe sixty-five, but then that all changed in 1996 when the assistant commissioners' retirement age was pushed down to sixty.

MF: They supported you in large numbers before the case....

MD: Oh, they did, yeah.

MF: And vanished into the woodwork after the case?

MD: A lot of them disappeared; a lot of them were hurlers on the ditch really. […] [O]h, I was going to be a great guy if I won it, but the old saying that success has many friends and failure is an orphan is quite true….

And the basis for the change in retirement age rankled with Donnellan, too.

MD: Well, in the document that I saw […] just a week before the case went for hearing, it was for dynamism and motivation. That was the central issue and to prevent blockages in the promotion line up along. Now, you know, I mean that's grand, and it sounds great, but there was no consultation, and there was no study done […]. [But] do you lose all your powers of motivation once you hit sixty, and do you lose your dynamism? That's the question that arises….

I mentioned to him the fact that judges and politicians don't have to retire at sixty. He added senior civil servants to the list, the people who wrote the legislation. He dismissed the notion of people "blocking the ranks" by staying on after age sixty, mentioning the fact that they had increased the retirement age of guards, sergeants and inspectors from fifty-seven to sixty in 2006: "Now, I didn't hear of any complaints about blockages in those ranks."

I had to ask Donnellan the obvious question.

MF: Now, there are some people who would say to you, "Martin Donnellan, are you [off your] trolley? You've put in forty years…."

MD: Sure.

MF: "You've got a good pension." "You're on half pay." And, some people would say, in the middle of a recession, "Happy days!"

MD: Oh, indeed. Happy days. That's true and, I mean, there's that side of it. Now, that's fine from an outsider's [point of] view, you know [...]. But, if you're inside, if you're inside on the job, you have a far different view of life, you know....

MF: You want to keep doing it.

MD: Well, yeah, I mean, at sixty you're not going to set the world on fire outside the Guards. I felt I had a lot to contribute and I genuinely felt that. [...] [L]ots of people go at fifty. People go at fifty-five. They go at sixty. Thirty per cent of senior officers go before they hit sixty for various reasons. Now, they may have family reasons, health reasons – there's a whole myriad [of reasons] – and people have different plans for later in life. My point in the whole thing was to have the choice. [...] This is 2008, [and it's] half a century [...] since they made the rules of retirement. [...] [W]e surely felt we'd be entitled to a choice. That was it in a nutshell....

MF: Because you loved the work.

MD: I loved the work. I got great job satisfaction. I worked with fantastic people in the Guards. I have nothing but the best wishes and everything for the Guards, you know. I mean, after forty years of service, you made great friends. I worked with very, very talented people in the Guards....

Donnellan's view on policing struck a slightly old-fashioned note – one that seems to hark back to a rural Ireland of bygone days. His character, formed by growing up in a tight-knit community, and his early years in the force clearly exerted a huge influence on how he worked and what he viewed as appropriate. His views chimed with those of many of our listeners. One listener called to say that when Donnellan was working as a young guard in Ballyfermot somebody had stolen his bike from outside the post office. Donnellan took off on foot, and ran the length of Ballyfermot to apprehend the thief and restore the bike to its owner.

MF: What makes a good guard, or what makes a good approach to solving a case?

MD: Well, you know, an old inspector said to me a long time ago when I was a young detective sergeant in the Bridewell [...]: "How are you getting on in here, sonny?"[...]. [W]ell, I said, "I'm getting on okay here, you know, but," I said, "a lot of this job is about common sense." He said, "Come in to my office." So he [took me into] the office. He was smoking a pipe, I'll always remember. He said, "Sit down there now, sonny. Close that door." [...] "Listen," he said, "when you're in this outfit as long as I am, you'll discover that common sense is not so common at all."

And that is so true, I mean, no matter what investigation you take on or how complex it appears to be, if you have a team – and I'd say this much: I was good at picking teams – if you have a team around you that is very talented first of all [...] and if they do the simple things well, I mean, that's what it's all about. It's [...] simple, policing is simple, but you need to be able to take full advantage of the half breaks, like any good football team or anything, the Kerry team or the Dublin team or, indeed, we had a very good Galway team one time and we still have a reasonably good team. […] Tull Dunne trained the Galway team and they won three All-Irelands in a row − […] I remember […] they were our heroes when I was growing up − and somebody asked Tull Dunne one day, "[H]ow did you win three in a row with this team?" [H]is answer was very simple. He said, "Well, I had a very talented bunch of players, but I got all those players to do the simple things exceptionally well." And that's what policing is about.

He went on to give a concrete example of what he meant.

MD: I was a detective sergeant in the Bridewell in about 1983 or 1984. I was there from 1980 to 1985. But there was a young girl – lovely – Denise Flanagan, found in a lane-way above in Stonybatter. Strangled. And we had nothing to go on from the start-off. Now, witnesses came forward and said they saw her at Rumours Nightclub on O'Connell Street the night before, and another witness who hadn't known her previously, remarkably, saw her getting into a taxi in O'Connell Street with a male. And we had a good descrip-tion of the male. Now, we then went about tracking the taxi, and I always remember there were checkpoints done in the Stonybatter area and Frank Hand − the Lord have mercy on Frank Hand who was shot dead at Drumree[9] a short time later − he found the taxi man and took in the taxi, took the seat covers off the taxi, and [we] were able to match the seat covers with Denise Flanagan's clothing. […]

[B]eside the body we'd found a pair of what we thought were sunglasses, and they were tinted glasses actually. They were prescription glasses got in an optician's. So […] we broke the team up into small teams and […] we went to every optician in Dublin and went to every optician in Leinster. And I remember going out to an optician who worked in the health place in Blanchardstown, and lived out in County Meath […]. [In an optician's], we'd go through the records if they allowed us, and most of them did because they were very busy, but this lady said, "You won't be able to make out my writing. I'll go through them with my husband at home." So she said, "Leave it with me." And I remember one night going home – and we were [in] this investigation […] for three or four months now – and I got a phone call from this lady and she said, "I have the prescription."

MF: What […] was your reaction to that?

MD: The hair stood on the back of my neck. I didn't want to get too excited, because […] maybe, you know, there'd be a couple of pairs of glasses with the same prescription. But [the optician had] said, "I remember the guy", and he was a good-looking, black-haired fellow, […] and he was from Blanchardstown.

[…] Tony Hickey was a detective sergeant or he was a detective inspector, I think, at the time, [and] he was on the team. They were down from the Murder Squad at that time, and we [decided not to] ring anyone that night. I said, "There's no point now in getting excited at half-ten at night time." There were no mobile phones or anything at that time. So, we met the following morning, and we took the guy in that day, and he admitted [to] the murder. And that was the most rewarding case, as regards investigating cases and attention to detail and [the] real foot-slogging that I was involved in. Now, I was involved in lots of cases, but that was one […] that stood out for me.

MF: [...] [W]hen you say, "Right, this is the right prescription. This is the guy", what goes through your mind at that stage and what about the approach to the guy?

MD: Well, [...] [y]ou couldn't hold people to question them at that time. So, it was all to do with the approach to this guy. How are we going to approach this fellow? And [what] is the most effective way of talking to him about it? So, I know the approach that we used anyway was that Tony Hickey [...] said, "Did you lose a pair of glasses, by any chance?" And he said, "I did. I did. Yeah. I lost them in Rumours Nightclub." [Tony] said, "I think you want to talk to me about a lot more than the glasses." [...] [A]nd he had practically admitted the thing before we were at the Garda station.

MF: Really?

MD: Yeah. [...] [N]ow we have Section 4, you can detain people and properly question them, but at that time there was a kind of an anomaly there and people were in Garda stations by invitation and all that type of thing, you know.

MF: Yeah, and what was his reaction when you knocked at the door?

MD: Well, we went to his place of work, actually [...]. We found out he was working up around Dorset Street. Well, he was a very cool customer. I mean he was very cool. [...] [W]e were wondering, "I wonder have we the right guy here?" [...] [B]ut then he was again subsequently identified on identification parades by the people who saw him leaving the nightclub with [Denise Flanagan]....

A bit later on, Martin elaborated a bit more on his views about policing and how it has changed throughout his career.

MF: And what's the reaction normally of somebody being arrested?

MD: Well, you know, I arrested and charged people for the most serious crimes in this country and I have to say that I would meet practically 95 per cent of them afterwards, after coming out of prison, and they'd come up and talk to me.

MF: Really?

MD: I mean that sincerely. [...] [Y]ou want to treat people with a bit of dignity. That's what I always found. It doesn't go astray. I mean, that would be my one [piece of advice] to our young guards today: listen, if a person was a criminal and all of it and then he stops crime and he's now married and he has a family and his young lad gets into trouble for some reason, the [...] biggest insult to that father when he comes into the station is [if you] treat him in an offhand way and say, "Well, what do you expect?" If you treat that man as a father, [and] bring him in, sit him down [and] say, "Listen, this young fellow's in trouble. We're going to try and we have to try and help him and we have to try and work this out [...]", you've a friend for life. I mean that and [...] I do think that we should get back to basics a little bit in this country with policing. Every guard in this country is [part of] a community. You know, you hear about this demarcation and all that. The detectives will be down if there's a house broken into. Sometimes they run or walk out the door again. That's wrong. I mean, they should take and show an interest and empathise with the poor woman in the house.

[…] I was on an interview board a couple of years ago with a lovely gentleman and he's retired from […] a different department, and his one complaint, would you believe, was, he lived up in Drumcondra, and when he walked up to get the paper, if he met a young Garda, he'd [say], "Good morning, Guard."[…] And he'd be highly insulted [because] sometimes, he said, a lot of them didn't reply to him. You know, that's a simple thing now, but I mean it would be a pity if we go away from that, you know.

The public of this country, I think, are very tolerant people. We have different types of crime now. We certainly have an aggressiveness in society that wasn't there when I joined the Guards forty years ago. We have that kind of aggressiveness where people are kicked on the ground and then, in the last three or four murder [cases] I saw, […] fellas […] went back to the house and got a knife and came back to the scene. Now, if anybody gets a knife or a firearm and approaches somebody, well, you know, they really mean to badly injure or kill that person, and, I mean, that's an aggressiveness that's crept into Irish society.

Donnellan mentioned that the advent of DNA testing had revolutionised the work of the Gardaí. But when I questioned him about how its use might, according to some, compromise individual rights, he didn't exactly address the issue.

MF: You're in favour of a DNA bank, aren't you?

MD: Very much so, yeah. I think […] [DNA testing] has been responsible for solving some major crimes here and I think, in this day and age, […] DNA should be part and parcel of everyday policing. There's no doubt about that.

MF: And what about the arguments about civil liberties and privacy and all that kind of thing?

MD: Well, you see, if you have a horrific murder in a district and you're left with very little, maybe only DNA, I don't see how people could object if there's some monster after savagely murdering and raping somebody. I think that the general public in Ireland are [...] very supportive and they're very law-abiding people, really. I mean, you know, there's tremendous support for the Garda Síochána across the country and, I mean, I think that that has been hard won by a lot of people who have gone before me, you know, and I'm not any different to lots of policemen. Okay, I was very privileged to have reached the rank I rose to....

One caller to the show posed a thought-provoking question: "Would you ask Martin why, if they can have him out of the Garda force, they find it so difficult to get rid of a bad egg out of the force?" And another chimed in with: "Could Marian ask Martin what does he think about the corrupt former Gardaí in Donegal who were found guilty under the Morris Tribunal,[10] and who have never served a day in prison, and are on a full Government pension?" In answer to the second question, Martin said:

MD: I think you know every member of the Garda Síochána [...] was saddened by Donegal. There's no doubt about that. I mean, some of the things that happened up there were ... I thought they were childish, to be honest with you....

MF: They were a bit stronger than childish....

MD: Well, […] I mean there was wrongdoing there and it was certainly highlighted, but this business about getting intelligence, or supposedly getting intelligence, and moving stuff around, I mean, […] it doesn't bear thinking about – and just for their own ends, or to make them look good…. That type of stuff. I mean, it beggars belief, to be honest with you. Now, some of the other stuff, like where wrongdoing was concerned, I mean, nobody in the Guards that I'm aware of would condone that kind of carry-on.

At the end of the interview, Donnellan talked with obvious regret about some high-profile cases that had not been solved. It struck me that he did so in a very human way. His concern seemed to be primarily about the victim and their loved ones – that he had somehow let them down – rather than about anything to do with Garda success rates. But he remained (characteristically) upbeat and hopeful that someday the cases will be solved.

MF: [Of] the other [cases] you've mentioned several times – there was Annie McCarrick and there was Raonaid Murray.[11]

MD: Yeah. […] I was [based] in Irishtown when Annie McCarrick went missing, and she had been staying in a flat in Sandymount, […] and I met her father and mother. [T]here's still bits and pieces being done with that [case]. Would you believe that?

MF: You still think, even after all these years, that these [cases] could be solved?

MD: Oh, it's still possible. Yeah. It is still possible, if the right break came; or, you'd be amazed, [...] a witness may come along who didn't think [their information] was important at the time. And people [have] come forward in relation to that in the not-so-distant past [...]. And there's a cold case review team now working from Harcourt Square, and they review murders that have gone cold, you know…that are a few years old, including Raonaid Murray's and that Annie McCarrick [case] that was, it was…

MF: It captured the whole country's imagination.

MD: It was really very sad, you know, for the parents. And she loved Ireland, and she saw no harm in any Irish people. [W]e know for certain she got a bus from Ranelagh because a lady saw her on the bus who knew her. Now, there were several other sightings, or supposed sightings, but she certainly got a bus which went towards [...] Enniskerry….

MF: Enniskerry.

MD: We could never positively say she was in Enniskerry, but certainly there's one witness [...] who was adamant that she was in Johnny Fox's [pub]….
    [...] Now, we couldn't push that any further. We pushed it as far as we could, but that's still live. And, I suppose, Raonaid Murray's [case] was the biggest disappointment to me, that we didn't get who did that. I think that was a horrific murder. An absolutely horrific murder. Lovely young girl, walking home from Dún Laoghaire and savagely stabbed, and her parents, and all parents, [...] were horrified. [...]

MF: Several times I've read that there were breakthroughs….

MD: Well, you know, there [were], but it was the one murder — I dealt with lots of murders in my career — but that was the one case, in all my career, that we never really got a real break, you know. You'll always get a phone call. You'll always get some piece of intelligence that somebody [knows] something or heard something and they [are] adamant that there's a real lead here. And that was the amazing thing about that investigation — we never got a [real break, even though] we had loads and loads of witnesses. […] I'd say, you know, it's still possible that [the case] might be solved. I hope it is.

11

Seán FitzPatrick, 04.10.2008

"I can't say sorry with any type of sincerity and decency..."

Seán FitzPatrick was once the poster boy of the Irish financial sector during the dazzling success of the Celtic Tiger years. As chief executive and later chairman of Anglo Irish Bank, he oversaw a period of unprecedented growth, based, largely, on loans to property developers in Ireland and the UK. There can't be a person in Ireland who is not well versed in the spectacular fall from grace of Anglo Irish Bank that followed the sharp downturn in the Irish property market in 2008. But there had been warnings: two years earlier, the economist David McWilliams had described the bank as "simply a leveraged hedge fund betting its own and its clients' money on overvalued property". The US subprime mortgage crisis and the collapse of Lehman Brothers greatly increased the bank's gross overexposure in an out-of-control property market.

In the weeks before Seán FitzPatrick agreed to be interviewed a palpable fear had grown throughout the country about what was happening in the financial markets. People were taking their money out of banks and trying to find somewhere safe to put it. Shares were rapidly losing value; pensions and investments had, in some cases, vanished. Scenes of depositors queuing outside the UK bank Northern Rock to withdraw their money were fresh in people's minds. I remember the story of one particular Northern Rock depositor, a woman who had sold her house and put the money on deposit, who was worried she might lose everything. Northern Rock was nationalised – it took us some time to realise how common nationalisation would become. In the mayhem, people in Ireland began to split their savings into multiple deposits of €20,000 – this was the amount guaranteed by the Irish Government. Joe Duffy, on RTÉ's *Liveline*, was accused of further destabilising financial markets when he clarified the guarantee situation. When the Government increased the guarantee to €100,000 things calmed down, but only temporarily. When the Financial Regulator Patrick Neary appeared on *Prime Time* to assure us all that the banks were solvent and well capitalised, few believed him.

Seán FitzPatrick originally agreed to come on the show as part of a panel to discuss the Irish Government's Bank Guarantee Scheme, which had been announced on 30 September. As the emergency legislation was pushed through the Dáil we got back in contact with him to see if he would be willing to do the Saturday interview instead. He agreed! Irish bankers were coming in for a real drubbing in the press and with ordinary punters at the time and we were sure he would pull out. One of the fears that

hangs over any broadcaster doing live interviews is that the interviewee will cancel at short notice. My producer Hugh Ormond
called him only to be told that, on the contrary, he intended to
show up and had feared that we would cancel on him!

When FitzPatrick arrived in the studio he was all chipper.
Listening to the interview again, it seems he genuinely believed
the answers he gave; his conviction never faltered, not even
once. In retrospect, it is apparent that FitzPatrick viewed the
interview as a public relations opportunity or at least a damage-
limitation exercise – an attempt to calm the speculation that we
were facing a complete meltdown of the Irish economy.

I began by asking him about the bank bailout, how he heard
about it and what role he played in it.

MF: Where were you on Monday night [29 September 2008]?

SF: […] I was out for dinner with a friend of mine so I got
home at around about half nine and watched TV and went
to bed around about eleven o'clock.

MF: And did you have any […] information about what was
happening?

SF: That particular night I knew lots of things were happening because we had discussions with the Central Bank and
with the Regulator and, indeed, with the Department of
Finance over the previous weeks. But that particular night I
was not aware of what was happening in detail.

MF: You didn't know what was happening?

SF: I didn't know what was happening in the sense that I didn't know that the meeting was taking place that night at ten or eleven o'clock. I knew there was a meeting at half four or five o'clock…But I didn't know that it was going on for so long.

MF: Well, when you went out for dinner, Anglo Irish shares were down on the day, what, 46 per cent?

SF: They were down 46 per cent, yeah.

MF: Did that afford any indigestion?

SF: Well, of course it did. I mean we were concerned, as indeed all the rest of the banks were. I suppose the big issue here is that if Anglo Irish Bank is down in isolation, you worry more, but all the banks were down that day in Ireland. All the banks were down in Germany. All the banks were down in the UK. So, there was a great sense that things were not moving in the right direction. I suppose….

MF: Did you see an Armageddon coming?

SF: Oh, I did. Yeah. I certainly was very, very concerned when I heard the news at dinner, indeed, that Congress hadn't voted on the $700 million [bailout]. At that stage, I really feared…and I…I've got to say to you, unashamedly, I was very fearful during the week.

MF: You know the rumour mill was flying around?

SF: Of course. That's Ireland.

MF: And they were saying that Anglo was the one.

SF: Well, you know Anglo is a very well-capitalised bank, but Anglo in line with all of the other Irish banks was in a situation where it was seeing global liquidity […] drying up….

MF: But you are on the record as saying that, largely speaking, you didn't borrow from other banks for your own loans, that you did it from a deposit base. You are on the record saying that on RTÉ.

SF: Yes, and that was the case.

MF: So it wasn't the liquidity thing that was your problem?

SF: It was a liquidity…I mean profitability is a, I won't say is a taken, but I mean you can see all the banks have been profitable over the last number of years and there was lots of talk and lots of rumour-mongers going around [talking] about the bad debts but, by and large, they were very profitable. […] The issue that faced all of the banks, Anglo Irish Bank and the other banks, was the drying up of the global wholesale markets, and when you realise….

MF: But you said you don't go to those wholesale markets, that you do it mainly from your deposit base.

SF: I said […] mainly from our deposit base, but of course you need this for liquidity, and our deposits, our loan-to-deposit ratio, is probably the best in Ireland at 125 per cent. So, of course we used that, but we used that as a top-up. And what we were finding then was that we had money that needed to be paid back over the course of the next few months and we were concerned about the liquidity and then where was the money going to come [from] for that? As, indeed, all of the banks were, as it subsequently came out….

FitzPatrick's two main agenda items recurred throughout the interview: the real issue was one of the drying-up of global financial liquidity; and Anglo Irish were no different to all the other banks. He seemed at pains to downplay any contact he might have had with senior politicians in the lead-up to the bailout, presumably to reinforce the impression that Anglo Irish Bank was no different to any of the other banks. He was adamant that the Government intervention was primarily about securing the Irish economy, and on a few occasions he suggested that the problem was one of perception – the press had made a bigger story out of it than it merited.

MF: If you didn't get it – the money that you needed – on the global market, how long would it have taken before you'd have been [in trouble]?

SF: Well, to quote the Taoiseach, which I read in the paper, we were all on the brink. It was very close….

MF: How close?

SF: Well, I mean it was a matter of days, I would have thought. That's why it was so important that Government acted so decisively and so boldly, and, you know, it was a bailout of the banks in a sense, but I mean it was a bailout for the Irish economy. The Irish economy, the Irish taxpayer must be grateful and we, the bankers, must be very grateful to the Government for what they did….

MF: Well, the first thing I would say is that you should be grateful…

SF: I'm sorry...

MF: And very few bankers came out to say thank you....

SF: Well, I'm saying thank you, unashamedly, because we owe our lives to the Government and what they did. Absolutely.

MF: Now, when you said the taxpayers should be grateful, I would suggest to you the taxpayer is deeply ungrateful....

SF: Now, sorry, can I just...?

MF: Because, can I say to you that if you ran a referendum on Monday to say, "Will we underwrite all this money with our hard-earned euro?", I don't think the referendum would have carried.

SF: Okay. Fair enough, Marian, and maybe you are right, certainly with all the publicity, but if I can just go through it in a very simple way why they should be grateful. If the Irish banking system had collapsed, there would have been chaos here and the real economy would have suffered and that would have affected you, Marian, your kids, my kids and all of our neighbours. We would have been in uncharted territory and anything could have happened – and I know bankers are not the favourite people for the past number of years – but it's very important in any democracy that we have a good banking system that provides the lubricant for the real economy. If [...] the Irish banking system had just exploded, then you don't know what would have happened. We could have actually been dominated by foreign banks and the big difficulty there is that they tend to pull back to their place of birth when there are difficulties and Ireland would then become the New Zealand of Europe. So, that's why it was so important that the Government acted.

Again and again, he asserted that Irish banks were the unwitting victims of the international financial crisis. And his answers became more and more oblique and circuitous.

MF: Why is every commentator, left, right and centre, saying that the Irish banks behaved imprudently, some would say recklessly, in the amount of money given and lent for property deals, when the dogs in the street, who don't own a house, knew that the property market was going down?

SF: Sure, okay Marian. I'll just deal with that in one second. But […] the global liquidity situation [must be divorced from] the rumours and speculation about property in Ireland. […]

MF: In June the investment bank Citigroup published a negative report on Irish banks, cutting its recommendation on Anglo Irish Bank from "hold" to "sell". […] The report said that 80 per cent of Anglo's loans are secured against Irish and UK commercial property.

SF: Okay, Marian. This is where the confusion comes in. They are investment reports about stock market holdings. Okay? And they are shareholders, recommendations to shareholders. We're not talking about the providers of liquidity and what was happening was there were no providers of global liquidity, and that was the big issue as to why the action took place last week, as to why the Irish Government had to take decisive and bold action on Monday night.

MF: Can I go back…?

SF: Now, I'll come to the issue of bad debts because [...] I've been reading the newspapers. I've been listening to the news. I've been watching TV and I've been speaking with friends of mine both in and out of banking. It's a common theme. And what you've got to understand is this: [...] when people say have we been reckless, of course banks have made mistakes. And Anglo Irish Bank has made mistakes and it has made mistakes in the past because we are in the business of risk and we have made mistakes and I'll admit that. Have we been reckless? No, we haven't. We cover all our loans in a belt-and-braces way. Ask any of our customers about that. So we don't believe we've been reckless.

MF: So, reports in the paper about €1.1 billion 100 per cent loans provided by Anglo, they're not true?

SF: I can't believe that we've ever given a 100 per cent loan in our lives. Anywhere.

MF: Ever?

SF: Ever.

MF: Or doing it in tranches so that it looks different?

SF: But, sorry, we're not trying to fool ourselves, Marian. I mean we're in the business of making money. We're business people and what we want to do is, we don't want to be reckless, we want to make money. In fact, you know, if I'd been sitting here with you two years ago, you would have been saying, "Look at all you guys! You're making all this money!" Now what you're turning around and sort of saying is, "You've been reckless and you're not going to make money."

MF: Well, the reason we're concerned about whether or not you've been reckless is that we're signing the Guarantee.

SF: Absolutely.

MF: So we have a vested interest now in ways that we, and by "we" I mean all the listeners, never had before.

SF: And, Marian, I agree fully and I think the world has changed since last Monday and I think, you know, as a chairman of a bank, we are going to have to take into account the views of the taxpayer in a way that we've never done before. This is a whole new paradigm, I think, for the boardrooms of Irish banks.

Another prime example of waffle was when I asked him about financial regulation.

MF: And what kind of input does the Regulator have in your lives?

SF: Well, he regulates very closely. He gets all of the information that he wishes to get from us in relation to our lending, in relation to our liquidity, in relation to our deposits and everything. He comes in, he does internal audits. He looks at the top twenty loans, forty loans. He gets information about various ratios, all of that. And the Central Bank will also get that type of information, if required, as well.

MF: Is that every quarter or....

SF: Yeah, every quarter and then any time they wish to make visits to all of the banks.

MF: Have they been doing a lot of visiting recently?

SF: Not recently, but, I mean, they have been doing consistent visits over the years and, I mean, they've been very mindful of the issue in relation to the growth in lending over the years and, particularly, in the growth of lending to home loans and mortgages and, indeed, in the growth of lending to developers.

FitzPatrick was very bullish in expressing the view that the banks should foot the bill for the bailout, one of his few statements that sounded a rare note of contrition. And, of course, in retrospect, the words ring particularly hollow.

MF: There is a certain irony, you might agree, that we have been preached at about "Let the market sort it out", "Let the market dictate", "The market will find its own weaknesses and strengths" and "The market should run it", and then, when the marketers get into difficulty, they go running to the Government and the taxpayer....

SF: [...] When they're talking about "Let the market decide", that means that the market can decide the valuations of banks. [...] The banks have dropped in value dramatically in Ireland since this time last year, over 70 per cent. That's what the value was and that's what the market says. However, we're not talking about the markets sorting out this problem, because this was a liquidity problem and there was nowhere else to turn to and, if Brian Lenihan and Brian Cowen had stood idly by to let the markets sort it out, we would have had chaos and we wouldn't be in the position which we are in today. Now, as regards the taxpayer, it is right that the banks should foot the cost of the Guarantee.

MF: How much [is the cost]? [...]

SF: I haven't spoken to the other banks and we haven't spoken to the Central Bank yet, and that will take place next week and our Chief Executive David Drumm....

MF: Have you not spoken to the other banks?

SF: Pardon? Have we not spoken to the other banks about the Bank Guarantee? Listen, a lot of things happened during the week and we were dealing with priorities, and the next priority will be actually dealing with the whole detail of what Mr Lenihan is proposing in the detailed Regulation. [...] And, much more importantly, if there is any bank that defaults, that default will be borne by the banking sector, in the first instance. So, all of the banks are going to have to go before the taxpayer is called on. And what we're really saying here is....

MF: Will you run that past me again. You were saying that, if one bank falls....

SF: [...] If a bank falls, that means that its liabilities are greater than its assets. Okay? So there's going to be a short-fall for the depositors. So someone is going to have to pay them. The Government has guaranteed them so they'll be paid. And then the Government will say, "Right, we've written a cheque for, I don't know, €200 million, €100 million", whatever the figure is — who's going to pick that up? That's not going to be the taxpayer; that's going to be borne by the rest of the banks. And that's quite clear and fully accepted by the banks, and rightly so. Of course it's right. So there's not going to be issues with that. So, what effectively the taxpayer has done is this: he's lent the Government's, the sovereign name of Ireland, to, particularly, outsiders that would feel that they can lend to Irish banks with a sovereign risk.

At another point in the interview FitzPatrick referred to the bailout as "probably the most important decision made in this country, from an economic point of view, since the foundation of the State" and seemed to genuinely believe that the crisis had been averted. It was FitzPatrick himself who raised the issue of "fat cat bankers".

MF: When will activity start?

SF: I think activity will start fairly quickly again. There was nearly paralysis over the last few months, so activity will resume when things calm down completely. [...] There's a certain theme, you know – the banks, my God! Big fat cat bankers ... Why are we not taking them all out? – [I] understand that completely, you know, absolutely understand that....But what we must understand is that is not just bailing out the bankers; it's ensuring that our economy, your economy, my economy, our kids' economy has a fair chance going forward.

MF: When they do get angry about "fat cat bankers", to use your own term, there is a bewilderment, not to mention anger, when you see people getting enormous bonuses on foot of appalling delivery. It seems there are decisions made to give pretty amazing bonuses no matter how people have performed.

SF: Well, first of all, I can only talk about our bank and I am very well aware senior Irish bankers are paid enormous sums in relation to the balance of the community. In our bank, we pay by performance. There's effectively a contract written out and agreed by, if you like, independent directors within the bank — who don't work in the bank, who work in different areas of the economy in Ireland — with the executives and that is agreed and, if the performance is reached, they get it. For instance, David Drumm's salary of last year, salary and bonus package — less than a third of that is basic salary and if he doesn't actually contribute and actually achieve his performance criteria, he doesn't get it. And it's as simple and as straightforward as that.

MF: But we were going down the tubes last week!

SF: But, sorry. Hold on. But we haven't paid anything this year, you know. So, I could just say to you and I will say to you very clearly that the boardrooms of Irish banks will have to take into account the views and wishes of the taxpayer, the new stakeholder in Irish banks, and I believe that that new view and that new paradigm will be reflected in the decisions that remuneration directors, i.e. the directors, independent directors that actually decide salaries, [make] to ensure that people are paid appropriately and not excessively.

MF: Will there be dividends this year?

SF: Will there be dividends this year? I can't say that to you in relation to Anglo Irish Bank because that would be wrong and inappropriate, but let me put it this way: the world hasn't stopped. We were talking about a liquidity problem. We weren't talking about a profitable problem and the banks will look at all of these. We've got to listen to the detail of what is going to be in the detailed Regulations next week and we're going to look at that and we're going to have to discuss this with the Central Bank and with the Department of Finance and reach a solution which is right, not just for the banks, but also for Government and the taxpayer.

Callers to the show were, as you can imagine, overwhelmingly hostile. One person said, "Now that the banker has said 'thanks', can he go the whole hog and say 'sorry' to the Irish people?"

> SF: Well, Marian, you know, it would be very easy for me to answer, you know, a call like that and say sorry. What I've got to say is this: the cause of our problems was global, so I can't say sorry with any type of sincerity and decency, but I do say a very genuine thank you, because that is right, I'm sure.

I suppose FitzPatrick performed exactly as you would have expected him to — deny all personal culpability, blame events beyond his control, claim that everyone was in the same boat, explain the Government intervention in terms of saving the Irish economy rather than the banks. And he was by no means a lone voice at the time — most of the Cabinet were, it seems, similarly deluded. Listening back to the interview with FitzPatrick, it feels like an imagined conversation with Chamberlain before World War II. So, I suppose, it was obvious that he would be less than forthcoming on reports of alleged insider trading by him and others in the weeks and months before the bailout was announced. After all, he was still the chairman of a bank that had been spectacularly successful in forging a new banking approach, and he still possessed enormous personal wealth.

> MF: There were headlines in the paper yesterday — mind you, they were also in the paper last Sunday — [...] about you and another director putting in...I think you put in €1.1 and

he put in €1.3 [million] into shares of Anglo Irish Bank, and they say now that there's going to be an investigation about insider trading.

SF: I saw that. I was very, very disappointed to see that story in the *Irish Independent* yesterday and I'll just tell you straight out there is no truth whatsoever in that story. None.

MF: Did you not have a sense that the Government was going to bail out the banks.

SF: No. I didn't have a sense.

MF: But you were talking to Brian Lenihan.

SF: Sorry. Sorry. Sorry. […] [L]ike other directors in the past, [I] was showing confidence in our shares by taking money at my own resources to buy shares in Anglo Irish Bank. It is the only way that I could articulate in a very clear way to a wide audience that I believed in Anglo Irish Bank and that's what I did. Now, I've been in banking thirty-five years. Clearly, I have to go through a process to actually get that cleared with our company secretary, with the chief executive of the bank, and that I did. There is no sense that there was anything done wrong.

MF: But did you not know beforehand that the Government was going to bail the banks out?

SF: Of course I didn't. That wasn't announced until Monday night.

MF: But you had been talking to the Minister the previous week?

SF: I'd been talking to the Minister [over] the previous ten days about various issues, about what he could do or what he might not do, but I wasn't sure what he was going to do.

The murky world of cosy deals between FitzPatrick, some of his fellow directors and others in the financial sector began to unravel not too many months after the interview. In December 2008 FitzPatrick resigned as chairman of Anglo Irish Bank, admitting he had hidden more than €80 million in personal loans from Anglo Irish shareholders. Three days later the Government recapitalised Anglo Irish with €1.5 billion. In January 2009 the bank was nationalised and the property developer Seán Quinn revealed that his family had lost €1 billion on risky Anglo stock deals – it subsequently grew to €2.8 billion. The following month the bank's annual report revealed loans of €451,000 to ten of its largest customers to buy its own shares, and the bank's headquarters was raided by fraud officers. In March 2010 FitzPatrick was arrested and released without charge, and later that year he was declared bankrupt. The Central Bank has estimated that the Anglo Irish bailout could eventually cost the Irish taxpayer €34 billion.

As FitzPatrick left the studio he seemed happy with the interview. Later, I noticed that he was doorstepped when he left the Radio Centre – he was the hated man of the moment that week, as he was to be so many times in the future, something I always feel is a bit unfair.

On a personal basis, for Seán FitzPatrick and his family it must have been a shattering experience. In the subsequent climate of fury and fear, you didn't hear too much sympathy for the man, ultimately just another human being who made some colossal mistakes for which we will pay. Seán FitzPatrick's fall from grace was so spectacularly public that he, maybe, saved the blushes of several other senior banking figures. Let us not forget that you, me and all the other taxpayers own percentages of Allied Irish Banks, Bank of Ireland and Irish Nationwide. What may not have fully sunk in with the listeners at the time of the interview was that that was the week when the banks' debts became the Irish sovereign debt. In the news headlines before the programme, by the way, we heard that our difficulties were likely to continue until 2009.

How innocent we all were then.

12

Richard Lewis, 27.03.2007

"My partner, my lover, my friend..."

I was part of the congregation in the church at Jim Greeley's funeral in late 2006 when something extraordinary happened. Jim's partner, Richard Lewis, was as far as I was concerned one of the shyest people on the planet; yet, such was his shock, grief and loss that he made his way to the altar to deliver one of the most moving tributes to a lost partner that I have ever heard.

All of my life I've known gay people and gay couples. Some have lived openly gay lives but others, particularly an older generation like Richard and Jim, were more discreet. Richard had been a guest on the show before, talking about his professional work as a fashion designer. Not long after the funeral, I approached him to see if he would be willing to come on the show and talk about his life with Jim – his partner of thirty-one years. He took very little persuading. Before he talked about Jim, I asked him about the realities of coming out:

MF: You didn't realise you were gay until you were thirty?

RL: Until I was thirty I'd met girls, and there was one particular girl. People always think being gay is just about sex. It's not. It's like being straight – it isn't just about sex. And I'd had no sexual problems with girls, but I couldn't make that final commitment. There was no girl that I met that I knew I wanted to spend the rest of my life with, and that's what I wanted. I met Jim and I didn't know he was gay because, again, he didn't broadcast it or he didn't hide it, and the subject just never came up.

MF: You were both working with the Samaritans?

RL: Yeah. To me at the time, being gay was like a sexual deviation, like S&M or bondage. I didn't realise that gay people fell in love, or had relationships. Now, that sounds stupid, somebody of thirty – but I was. And as I got to know [Jim], I just realised I was looking forward to meeting him and we started meeting quite a lot, and then he asked me to take him for a driving lesson, which I did. I warned him, "Now, you have to be very careful and take it very slowly", but, of course, after about five minutes he started shooting around the Phoenix Park and [afterwards I] got out of the car and my knees were wobbling. I said, "I need a drink" and we had a few drinks and they went straight to my head and then it hit me. I said, "I actually love this guy."

MF: And what did that mean for you, Richard?

RL: Shock. Oh, I was horrified! I ended up with a psychiatrist. I did not want to be gay. Now, I don't think anybody chooses it. And I was having counselling and they said, "We can't tell you if you're gay or straight; we can only help you make up your mind." [...] I thought [...], "Ah, no. I've got to sort this out myself and why am I running away from something I love?"

MF: And why? Was it because of social isolation?

RL: Yeah. Society didn't accept it then, but, I think, probably accepted it more than I realised. I thought, "No. It's fine for somebody else to be gay, but not for me." And then I realised, "Why run away from somebody you love?"[...]

So, it was a six-foot-tall guy with a black moustache, rather than a five-foot-four girl with blonde hair, and I realised that he was the one I wanted.

MF: Were you ashamed of it?

RL: Perhaps, yes. At the very beginning I didn't tell any friends, but friends copped and, I think, maybe some friends copped before I copped. [...]

And it was just accepted and it was a few years before I actually verbalised [it] to my friends and they said, "Yeah. Fine. So, you know, you love each other. That's grand."

I originally met Richard at his studio where I'd gone to have a fitting. I needed something to wear for a public event – I can't remember what the occasion was – and a friend had told me that Richard's clothes were both practical and stylish. They were right; I had that outfit for years. On the rare occasions when I visited his studio Jim would be there and, of the two, he was the more gregarious – he exuded energy and warmth. He was a big bear of a man, who you immediately liked and trusted. He was full of good humour, a person who would do you a favour if he could. I remember one Christmas meeting him carrying an enormous holly wreath that he had bought for a song on O'Connell Street. I expressed great admiration and some envy for his purchase, while explaining how much I hate Christmas shopping fever. A few hours later he called me to say he had bought a wreath for me and could I come and collect it. It was a small gesture, but very indicative of the man.

Of course, I also liked that he was a great radio listener and often expressed great compassion for people who would tell their story of this or that difficulty in their lives. It was easy to imagine him as a Samaritan; as mentioned in the interview, he and Richard had met while working for the organisation. I was shocked when I heard of his death.

Richard was still grieving deeply when I interviewed him. His description of the manner of Jim's death, and the immediate aftermath, was particularly affecting:

RL: He had left for work at a quarter to seven and the Guards arrived at ten past eight. He had dropped dead in the street....

MF: Massive heart attack?

RL: Massive heart attack. No history. No nothing. And one guard sat down with me and chatted with me to find out what the situation was. The other guard went out and made a cup of tea for me and then they said, "Well, he's your partner — fine." So, as far as they were concerned, I was next of kin. [...]

Then the hospital was exactly the same. The consultant came down and he — at this stage, I was with Jim's sister-in-law — and the consultant said, "Who's next of kin?" And before I could say anything, Jim's sister-in-law, Phil, just turned to me and said, "Richard is." So, there were no problems there at all.

Apart from dealing with the loss of his partner of thirty-one years, Richard was confronted with a situation in which he could have been completely sidelined or ignored. As he said himself, he had no automatic rights as next of kin. I recall the pain of a woman who spoke to us on radio about the dying, death and funeral of her partner of many years. At the hospital, the family did not want her there and the medical staff would only deal with the next of kin. After her partner lost consciousness she was barred from the bedside. She was not consulted about the funeral and sat at the back of the church, heartbroken, shunned and excluded. And it didn't end there – there were the money worries, inheritance tax issues, the question of assets held in common. Richard was luckier than that woman, but nobody should be dependent on luck. Until Charlie McCreevy, as Minister for Finance, changed the rules for co-habiting couples, it was not unusual for someone to have to sell their home to pay inheritance tax when a partner died – he or she was classed as a "stranger-in-law".

MF: Again, there's a problem about legal rights, isn't there?

RL: Not with the house. I was told about four weeks ago, somebody said to me, "By the way, if one of you" – before Jim died – "if one of you dies, you'll have to pay inheritance tax on your home." But, in actual fact, Charlie McCreevy changed the law recently.[12]

MF: That's right.

RL: So the home is safe but any money Jim left, I have – if civil unions had come in I [would be] fine – but I will have to pay tax on [it]. I'm allowed €26,000 and [above that] I have to pay tax on everything.

MF: Even though it's something you created together.

RL: Yeah. And any joint accounts – I have to pay tax on half. [...] Even though tax has already been paid. But, I mean, it's money I don't have... [but] that doesn't bother me.

MF: In the order of priorities?

RL: Yes. But, I mean, I hope things change because there could be other couples, and female couples as well, in situations where tax could prove to be a big problem. [...] I gather it's on the way to being changed.

Shortly before Richard did the interview, the then Polish President Lech Kaczyński said that the human race would disappear if homosexual lifestyles were promoted on a large scale. His comments were roundly denounced on all sides. There has been a huge sea change in attitudes to gay people in Ireland since homosexuality was decriminalised in 1993 by a Fianna Fáil–Labour coalition government – in response, I might add, to the case taken to Europe by Senator David Norris. Fianna Fáil tended to be pragmatic about the introduction of progressive legislation when it had little choice – the kind it traditionally opposed when in opposition. However, Máire Geoghegan-Quinn, the Minister for Justice who introduced the legislation, appeared to be a genuine conviction politician. In 2010, when civil partnership passed into law, it was broadly supported by all political parties and the general public. Even those who felt uneasy seemed resigned to the fact that official recognition for co-habiting same-sex couples was inevitable.

I had always presumed that Richard and Jim were gay and partners. I didn't care much one way or the other. And yet, in a metropolis like Dublin, it's easy but wrong to be blasé. Gay men and women, until relatively recently, lived lives that were outside the law. They were often socially excoriated and subjected to casual insults of the crudest and cruellest kind, not to mention violence, including murder. Richard always struck me as a very private and shy person. Years before, when I had interviewed him about his career and work, I remember he was careful to avoid anything personal. And, yet, at Jim's funeral, he felt compelled to give a moving tribute from the altar about Jim and their life together, and how they would have liked to be able to have a civil partnership.

MF: You said yourself at his funeral that he was your partner, your lover, your friend, and I think it was very difficult for you to do that. Was that the first time you had said something like that in public?

RL: I had never spoken [about our relationship] in public in my life. I can do an interview no problem, one to one. I had never spoken in public. I couldn't do it, but, I don't know, I was on autopilot and I arranged the priest, who was an old friend, who we knew before he became a priest, so he was a late vocation; so he has his two feet on the ground and he knows what life's about. [...] And then a few people offered to say a few words and I thought, "No. That'll drag things on. That's not what he'd want." And I said, "I'll say something." And my friends were going, "What? Richie's gonna talk?" And I did. I didn't find it difficult because I was in shock and I had to do it. [...] And when you have to do something, you do it.

MF: But you also said that you would have liked to have gotten married. Would you have gotten married?

RL: Oh. Yes. Yes. But I also opened by saying civil unions haven't come in yet. And a piece of paper doesn't make a difference. We would have had a civil union for legal reasons. Because, if Jim were ill, had been ill, I had no rights, you know. You have no rights at all and it's for that we would have done it. [...]

At another point in the interview I pushed Richard on stereotyping of gay people and how discrimination is far from a thing of the past.

RL: I think it's going. I remember talking to a taxi driver and the subject came up that I was gay and he said, "Tell me, why do all gay men carry on like women and do this and that and the other?" And I said, "Why are all straight men chauvinistic and aggressive?" It's not true. [...] [A] certain number of straight men are chauvinistic, aggressive, but not every man.

MF: This is true.

RL: And the same applies to gay men. [But maybe certain gay men acted in a certain way] [...] because they had to.

Gays had to get together because they weren't accepted anywhere else.

MF: I was listening this morning to a discussion about what's happening in Poland, where the President is turning on gay people [...]. And all down through the years, there have been some really [...] crude and savage things said about gay people. Did that hurt personally, or could one live one's life without feeling demeaned by it?

RL: Personally, I've never had anything happen to me that was anti-gay. [...] Never. But, as you say, [...] I think things are changing. [...] Hopefully. I remember a friend of mine [...] – he's an academic, and the subject came up – [...] sent me a book by courier to read [...][about] gay marriages in the Christian church up until the twelfth century...And [...] there were different ceremonies for heterosexual couples, for male couples and for female couples, and it's not that new and [...] at least 10 per cent...

MF: Of the population [are gay].

RL: Yeah. I don't think about it much. I'm surrounded by friends. I've never had personal problems with friends.

Richard was particularly frank about his grief, as well as the much more mundane reality of adjusting to life without a business partner who seemed to manage each and every part of his life.

RL: For the moment I have to do what Jim did before and it takes me three times as long to do it. [...] Plus, I still do what I normally do as well.

MF: And loneliness?

RL: Loneliness is starting to sink in now. I was in shock for the first month and then I just went numb for a month and now I'm sort of coming back to normal [...]. I didn't cry until about two weeks ago. I cried two days after our [fashion] show. I couldn't cry and I'm a great believer in crying because it just gets everything out and it helps you deal with [things], but I was just frozen. But loneliness, yes, and loneliness I'm now feeling in work because I'm about to say, "I'll get Jim to do something" – and he's not there. [...]

And [I'm] doing things at home that he would normally do, like I didn't know how to put out the rubbish bins and there are about ten. [...]

Yeah and hopefully, hopefully the pain will go, the sadness will go, but I hope the love doesn't.

MF: Could you ever see yourself getting involved with somebody again?

RL: No.

Notes

1 The advert showed Mary O'Rourke, who was Minister for Public Enterprise at the time, in a bubble bath and accused the Minister of "minding the Aer Rianta monopoly".

2 In the 2009 Republic of Ireland vs France World Cup qualifier, the French captain Thierry Henry's illegal handball, which was missed by the referee Martin Hansson, led to the decisive goal being scored by France. France qualified for the World Cup at Ireland's expense.

3 In actual fact, the figure negotiated by Albert Reynolds with the then European Community in Structural Funds was in the region of €7 billion.

4 *Bungalow Bliss*, Jack Fitzsimon's 1971 book of house plans, was a runaway success in Ireland – it ran to eleven editions. The book provided a set of readymade design modules aimed at the self-build market or amateur architect. It is often cited as being single-handedly responsible for destroying much of the Irish landscape.

5 *Yes Minister* is a satirical British sitcom set in Whitehall. It was produced by the BBC and ran for thirty-eight episodes in the 1980s.

6 Keane's career to date: he played for Cobh Ramblers (1989–1990); Nottingham Forest (1990–1993); Manchester United (1993–2005); and Celtic (2005–2006). Internationally, he played

for the Republic of Ireland for fourteen years and was captain of the Irish team. He has managed Sunderland (2006–2008) and Ipswich Town (2009–2011).

7   S.I. No. 16/1996 Garda Síochána (Retirement) Regulations: "Notwithstanding anything in the Garda Síochána (Retirement) Regulations, 1934 (S.R. & O., No. 146 of 1934), as amended, and the Garda Síochána (Retirement) (No. 2) Regulations, 1951 (S.I. No. 335 of 1951), as amended and the Garda Síochána (Retirement) Regulations, 1990 (S.I. No. 318 of 1990), a member of the Garda Síochána appointed to the rank of Assistant Commissioner or Deputy Commissioner after the commencement of these Regulations shall retire on attaining the age of 60 years."

8   Imelda Riney was an artist living in a remote part of Co. Clare. She was murdered, along with a local priest and her three-year-old son, in 1994.

9   Detective Garda Frank Hand was murdered during an IRA post office raid in Drumree, Co. Meath in 1984.

10 The Morris Tribunal was established in 2002 to investigate allegations of corruption in the Garda Síochána in Co. Donegal.

11 Annie McCarrick was a New Yorker living in Sandymount, Dublin. She went missing in Ireland in 1993. A witness claimed to have seen her at Johnny Fox's pub in the Dublin mountains, which is the last reported sighting of her. Raonaid Murray was stabbed to death in 1999 in Dún Laoghaire, Co. Dublin.

12 In 2006 the Minister for Finance, Charlie McCreevy, amended the law applying to inheritance tax so that if a person died their house could be inherited by any person who had lived with them in that house, as a principal primary residence, for at least three years prior to the death of the owner, regardless of their relationship.